The faith of the Vatican

The faith
of the
Vatican
A fresh look at Roman Catholicism

Herbert Carson

With much love

Dad.

 EVANGELICAL PRESS

EVANGELICAL PRESS
12 Wooler Street, Darlington, Co. Durham, DL1 1RQ, England

© Evangelical Press 1996
First published 1996

British Library Cataloguing in Publication Data available

ISBN 0 85234 345 0

Printed and bound in Great Britain at the Bath Press, Avon.

Contents

Preface

Truth is very precious. John introduced his Gospel by pointing to Jesus as the one who was 'full of grace and truth' (John 1:14). Jesus emphasized that when he spoke of himself as 'the truth' (John 14:6). He spoke also of its liberating power: 'You will know the truth, and the truth will make you free' (John 8:32). He designated the Holy Spirit, whom he would send to take his place after his ascension, as 'the Spirit of truth' (John 16:13). By contrast he spoke of Satan as 'a liar and the father of lies' (John 8:44). The apostle John echoed this evaluation of the work of the Holy Spirit: 'The Spirit is the truth' (1 John 5:7). He added further: 'No greater joy can I have than this, to hear that my children follow the truth' (3 John 4). It is no surprise therefore to find Paul setting truth as the foremost theme for meditation: 'Whatever is true ... think about these things' (Phil. 4:8). There is a like emphasis in his urging Timothy to aim at being 'a workman who has no need to be ashamed, rightly handling the word of truth' (2 Tim. 2:15).

But truth can be very uncomfortable! It demands not only assent but action. The Holy Spirit uses the truth to probe our consciences and then to stir our wills to response. When therefore we use the truth as the criterion by which the church is to be tested, we must react if the truth detects and displays serious flaws. Truth then challenges us to do something about

them. Many Christians have struggled at this point as they
have faced the question: 'Can I with consistency remain
within a church when I have a major disagreement with
fundamentals in its creed?' I speak with deep feeling as I
myself faced that challenge over thirty years ago. Should I aim
at reform within the existing structure, or did conscience
demand consistency with such painful persistence that I had
no alternative but to leave what had been the church of my
upbringing and the church of my family and forebears? This
deeply painful experience has given me sympathy for many
Catholics struggling with these issues. The fact that I was a
clergyman of nearly twenty years' standing has led to what I
trust is a realistic concern for Catholic priests facing the same
traumatic decision. In this spirit of shared concern I invite you
to read this book, with truth as the criterion and the Holy Spirit
as the guide.

1.
Catechism of the Catholic Church

11 October 1992, the date chosen for the launch of a historic publication, was a most significant occasion for Roman Catholics and, indeed, as the preface to the catechism makes clear, for all who either aim at church unity or simply want to know what the Catholic Church believes.

In the first place, the date was significant because it marked the thirtieth anniversary of the opening of the Second Vatican Council. The catechism was thus intended to draw together the documents of that council, and to provide an up-to-date presentation of its teaching.

Another factor which added to the significance of this publication was its recollection of the catechetical summary of the teaching of the Council of Trent known as the creed of Pope Pius IV. The Council of Trent, which was Rome's great reply to the Protestant Reformers, ended in 1563. The next year saw the production of the creed which has sometimes been called the 'Tridentine Profession of Faith'.

There have, of course, been a number of local catechisms and a long series of papal edicts, encyclicals and bulls. This catechism, however, represents the first comprehensive statement of Roman Catholic beliefs for more than four centuries. It can thus claim to be a landmark in the history of Catholic teaching. The parallels between the new publication and the

Council of Trent are also significant in that in each case the creed and the catechism purport to echo and expound the teaching of a major ecumenical council.

There is, however, a great contrast between the period when the creed of Pope Pius IV appeared and the present. The sixteenth century had seen the great disruption of Catholicism with Luther's and Calvin's challenges and the emergence of the reformed churches. There was a head-on collision between two diametrically opposed ways of understanding the Christian faith. The Council of Trent was thus a militant gathering aiming to consolidate the battered ranks of Rome and to attempt to see off these Protestant heretics, as they were viewed. Hence the statements at Trent were undergirded by vigorous denunciations of any dissenters. *'Anathema sit'* ('Let him be accursed') was the frequently repeated dismissal of the Reformers and their teaching.

The Second Vatican Council struck a very different note. When Pope John summoned the council he not only invited the prelates from the worldwide Roman church, but also observers from other churches who had now moved from being heretics or schismatics to being referred to as 'separated brethren'. His welcoming approach was somewhat qualified, though such was the ecumenical euphoria that it was seen as a generous gesture. In fact a careful reading of the papal document *Ad Petri Cathedram* will discover that what was being called for was a return to Rome. The tone may be friendly but the message is clear: true unity can only be realized when there is submission.

The current scene

Thirty years on there has been much progress down the ecumenical path. What is strikingly different is that there seem to be changes in Rome — the operative words here are 'seem to be'! At the same time there has been a markedly different attitude among evangelicals, especially in Britain and North America. Increasingly there have been joint enterprises in the area of evangelism. There has been joint participation in charismatic gatherings. Many evangelicals who formerly saw Rome as a bastion of doctrinal error, and Roman Catholic countries like Latin America as a fruitful area for evangelism, now view Roman Catholic and evangelical churches as co-operating in the common sphere of evangelizing the world.

1994 saw not only the English translation of the catechism but also the production of a joint statement by evangelicals and Roman Catholics which would have been utterly inconceivable even a few years ago. Those who had been meeting together since 1992 to produce the statement of united endeavour, and those who lent their names in support of the document, included prominent evangelicals whose names would be well known on both sides of the Atlantic. They came from denominations such as the Assemblies of God, the USA Southern Baptists, seminaries like Wheaton College and Fuller, and inter-denominational bodies such as Campus Crusade, the World Evangelical Fellowship and the Prison Fellowship. Obviously the contributors speak as individuals and the churches from which they come are not necessarily committed to their views. Indeed many of these bodies would repudiate the joint statement. Yet it is clear that those involved represent a very wide spectrum.

These people have moved on from their initial co-operation in the anti-abortion movement. But then many Christians have been involved in pro-life work without seeing such participation as in any way an ecumenical endeavour. After all, the anti-abortion attitude is common not only to a wide band of Christians, but to many who are not Christians at all and who would heartily disclaim any suggestion that they were.

This joint statement, however, takes us far beyond the area of social co-operation. It is a call rather for a united enterprise in evangelism and an end to what it terms proselytizing — that is, endeavouring to reach and win those who are nominal adherents of another ecclesiastical group.

This might all be dismissed as merely a misguided attempt by a group of individuals who must therefore not be taken too seriously, However, the situation is not so straightforward. In fact this statement represents an attitude which is becoming more widespread among evangelicals. Increasingly there is talk of recognizing Rome as a true church and Roman Catholics as partners in the area of evangelizing a godless world.

Nor is this conciliatory attititude confined to evangelicals. There is an increasing body of opinion within Rome which would not wish to have the term 'evangelical' restricted to non-Roman Catholic bodies. Indeed, those who subscribe to this view would be glad to use the term themselves and designate themselves as evangelical Catholics. Others involved in the charismatic renewal movement would take a similar line. So we are facing a new alignment of forces in an increasingly confused church situation.

The importance of the new catechism

The *Catechism of the Catholic Church* is of special significance in this discussion. It demonstrates very clearly that Rome has in no way modified the teaching of the Council of Trent. The tone may be friendlier, and the presentation more acceptable to late twentieth-century readers, yet the decrees of Trent are still there. Of course, there is teaching which is not found in the creed of Pope Pius IV. The council members at Trent had not heard of several doctrines which had yet to be invented when they met. It would be around three centuries before the dogmas of the immaculate conception of Mary and of the infallibility of the pope would appear. It would be another century before the formulation of the doctrine of the assumption of Mary and, later on, that of her motherhood of the church. So the changes in the catechism are not modifications of Trent, but additions to it coupled with reinforcement of its teaching.

One might quote at length from the catechism to show how closely it agrees with the findings of Trent. However, it may suffice by way of illustration to make a brief reference to three areas of agreement — namely transubstantiation, justification by faith and purgatory. On the issue of the real presence the catechism quotes directly from Trent: 'In the most blessed sacrament of the Eucharist "the body and blood together with the soul and divinity of our Lord Jesus Christ and therefore the whole Christ is truly really and substantially contained".'[1] On justification there is again complete agreement that 'Justification is not only the remission of sins, but also the sanctification and renewal of the interior man.'[2] On purgatory there is a like agreement. In fact the catechism affirms that 'The Church formulated her doctrine of faith on Purgatory especially at the Councils of Florence and Trent.'[3]

The pope gives his own personal and authoritative endorsement in the preface to the catechism. Those who are familiar with traditional Roman Catholic teaching will find it all here. The appeal of Trent to Scripture and tradition is firmly underscored. Papal infallibility is strongly reasserted. Baptismal regeneration — that is, the view that the child receives spiritual new birth in baptism — is a constant refrain. So too is the teaching of transubstantiation, the claimed miraculous change of the substance of bread and wine into the actual body and blood, soul and divinity of Christ himself. This is coupled with the notion of the eucharist as a sacrifice. Purgatory also, with its allied doctrine of indulgences, is still here. Above all,

there is a tremendous emphasis on the rôle of Mary in the work
of salvation. That emphasis colours the pope's preface, which
ends with earnest prayer to Mary to assist the ministry of the
catechism.

Thus the catechism has a message for any Roman Catholics
who may be tempted to give a very qualified acceptance of
some of their church's dogmatic teaching. Those who are
closely involved in ecumenical enterprises and those who
would claim to be 'evangelical Catholics' are particularly in
view here. There is no room for liberal theology, with its
reduction of the supernatural to a more rationalized reinterpretation. Neither is there justification for those who display a
reticence in the united prayer group where invocation of Mary
would be an alien idea. Such Catholics are given a fresh
reminder of Cardinal Hume's comment on Anglican seceders
that Rome does not present an à la carte menu! There can be
no picking and choosing. There must be full and unqualified
acceptance. Otherwise it would be dishonest to claim to be a
Roman Catholic since to accept only what one chooses would
be to violate one of the most basic tenets of Rome — that individual judgement must give way to the authority of the church.

The catechism also speaks very clearly to evangelicals who
are in danger of blurring the distinctives of the gospel in their
attempt to accommodate within a prayer fellowship those
Roman Catholics whom they recognize as brothers and sisters
in Christ. What such people need to realize is that it is no act
of charity to leave a fellow Christian in a state of error, when
we have the opportunity, and indeed the responsibility, of
correcting that error. When Peter lapsed into error at Antioch
Paul did not argue that since Peter was a brother in Christ, and
had been greatly used by God to reach others with the gospel,
therefore it would be a breach of loving fellowship to correct
him. In fact Paul was firm and open and told Peter he was
wrong (Gal. 2:11).

Paul's concern was for the purity of the gospel and so he could not let a loving relationship lead him to condone error. To argue that if we share with others a love for Jesus, we should therefore turn a blind eye to very grave doctrinal error, is to run completely contrary to Scripture. Indeed, it does despite to the very fellowship which is supposed to be enhanced. It is a shallow fellowship indeed that allows toleration of false doctrine. It is a strange love that does not try to point someone to a truer and more secure path.

Controversy or controversialism?

There is a widespread assumption that there are only two alternatives: either a flabby accommodation with error in order to promote a warm relationship or, on the other hand, a strident Protestant bigotry whose success is measured in decibels and whose writing seems steeped in vitriol. I recall a comment I heard years ago that the Christian is called to be the salt of the earth, not the caustic soda! It is, however, a perfectly biblical activity to engage in controversy. If the truth is valued then we have a duty to defend it. But a controversial spirit is totally different. It suggests a constant readiness to pounce and indeed, at times, almost a delight in the existence of error as an opportunity to exercise one's debating skill!

Certainly Jesus himself was controversial and was prepared to speak clearly, incisively and indeed bluntly, in order to deal with the propagation of error or the twisting of the truth for personal advantage. But the negative approach which controversy involves was not his primary aim. Rather he was in the first place the positive presenter of God's truth. The negative side was secondary, but it was none the less necessary. Similarly, the apostle Paul could flash with righteous indignation as he countered false teaching which would subvert the faith of believers. But his primary goal was not controversy but the declaration of truth, whether to religious Jews or to godless Greeks.

Speaking personally, I have found it possible to debate with Catholic priests and theologians and to avoid rancour. I recall a lecture given in a Roman Catholic seminary where I spoke on the defects in Rome's view of the way of salvation. The warm response was not because there were no attacks on Catholic dogma — there were! Nor was it because we were submerged in ecumenical politeness. It was, I believe, because there were many young students for the priesthood who were perplexed by the turmoil in their church and confused by the welter of conflicting views.

It has not been my aim in this book to win a clever argument and to overwhelm my opponents. That would indeed be a sterile exercise! I have tried rather, perhaps not always successfully, to remember the admonition of the apostle Paul, that doughty combatant in the cause of truth: 'Have nothing to do with stupid, senseless controversies; you know that they breed quarrels. And the Lord's servant must not be quarrelsome but kindly to everyone, an apt teacher, forbearing, correcting his opponents with gentleness' (2 Tim. 2:23-25). My aim in the chapters which follow is to conduct the controversy in that spirit.

2.
History teaches us!

The Christian, of all people, should never dismiss history as unimportant or irrelevant. To ignore the past is to be liable to repeat past errors. To forget the glory of past years is to lose a great source of encouragement when the going is hard. Above all, we cannot but profit from the realization that history displays the providence of God, who takes both good men and evil men, both prosperity and suffering, both peace and war, and all the varied events which are the story of the past, and weaves all the diverse elements into a pattern which will, in the final analysis of eternity, declare the glory of the sovereign God.

This is not only true for individuals but for churches. To reflect on a church's past history is to be challenged as we encounter a great galaxy of godly men and women whose lives remain a source of rebuke and challenge when a church lapses into complacency. Similarly, to see how the church faced persecution, how she allowed error to corrupt the truth and accepted lower standards, how God blessed her with spiritual awakening and chastened her in days of spiritual drought — all this and much more will surely compel us to acknowledge that an awareness of the past is a spur to progress in the present.

The early years

When Jesus was born in Bethlehem the country was occupied by the legionaries of imperial Rome. As in a great number of nations across Europe and North Africa, the emperor in Rome was the supreme ruler. Roman rule, of course, brought advantages in terms of social stability, education and culture. It also brought the wonderful system of roads facilitating safe travel. It presented to the first Christians an enormous challenge as the clash developed between the officially sanctioned religion of the empire and the claims of Christ to be the only Lord.

The Roman empire was very accommodating as far as religion was concerned. The religion of classical Rome included a great variety of gods and goddesses. When a nation was conquered its deities would also be taken over and added to the list of acceptable religions. The Christians would similarly have been accommodated if they had been prepared to accept inclusion in the religious conglomerate that was Rome. The trouble was that Christians made exclusive claims. They insisted that Jesus was uniquely 'the way, the truth and the life'. To embrace the gospel was to reject the whole galaxy of pagan deities. Above all, it meant rejecting the quasi-divine status of the emperor. For the average Roman citizen it was little more than a civic duty to offer a pinch of incense at the emperor's shrine. It didn't commit you to believing in the cult of the emperor, any more than pagan shrines committed many sceptical Romans whose acceptance of the worship of the various deities was purely nominal. To belong to your trade guild meant outward conformity and for many it was part of normal living.

For the Christian it was totally different. To say, 'Jesus is Lord,' was for them an uncompromising confession. It ruled out any kind of sharing in pagan worship. Above all — for this was a dangerous step to take — they could not say, 'Cæsar is Lord.' It was this nonconformity which led to social ostracism and to great hardship when they were excluded from their trade guild whose festival was celebrated in a pagan temple. It led finally to harsh persecution which persisted intermittently for the first three centuries of Christian history.

Those were years when great numbers of martyrs paid the supreme penalty. They were imprisoned, tortured and killed. Often their deaths were a spectacle laid on in the arenas of Rome to satisfy the blood-lust of a degenerate population. Yet in spite of the suffering the gospel still prevailed. It was then that the saying was coined by Tertullian that 'The blood of the martyrs is the seed of the church.' Far from silencing the church's witness, persecution was an incentive to press on with the commission to preach the gospel to every creature. Every stratum of Roman society was penetrated. Then, suddenly, the whole situation was dramatically changed.

Christianity becomes the religion of the state

In A. D. 311 Constantine was making his final bid to seize the imperial crown. The battle of the Milvian bridge was the decisive victory which put Rome and the throne of the Cæsars in his hands. The night before the battle Constantine claimed to have seen a vision of the cross in the sky with the words: *'In hoc signo vinces'* ('By this sign you will conquer'). The outcome was his granting of legal status to the church. It was the beginning of a very different chapter in Christian history. From being a persecuted sect the church became under Constantine's successors the church of the empire. Christians moved into positions of power. The glory of the martyrs and confessors was exchanged for the lustre of a religious establishment enjoying imperial favour.

The cost of acceptance proved in the long term to be very great. Formerly to be baptized was to risk torture and death. Now it became the accepted pattern of Roman life to be a

Christian. Pagans flooded into the churches in great numbers. Indeed, it was paganism which became unfashionable and ultimately was forbidden. The developing pattern was the incorporation of every family into a version of Christianity which made it the church of the nation. To be born again had been the basic requirement but now birth into a family ensured acceptance. There was already an existing ceremony in Rome to celebrate the birth of a baby. The ceremonial washing in water was accompanied by the giving of the *praenomen*, the first name. It was easy to give the ceremony a Christianized interpretation. When the practice became a legally binding requirement an even more serious situation arrived. In A. D. 529 the Emperor Justinian issued his *Body of Civil Law (Corpus iuris cvilis)* in which fines and banishment were imposed for baptizing those who had been christened in infancy. The way was clear for the developing of the doctrine of baptismal regeneration — 'I became a Christian when my name was given.' This was explicitly taught ultimately by the Council of Trent.

Missionary outreach had always been, from the days of Christ's commission to his disciples, the life-blood of the church. Now, however, the new pattern produced the sacral society — that is, the situation where church and state are two aspects of the same coin. So the aim in view became the winning of the chief or king, with his people following with what was a very nominal attachment. The next step was the enforced conversions by a victor in war as a matter of policy aiming at the subjugation of a conquered people. When Charlemagne defeated the Saxons the alternatives faced by the conquered Saxons were baptism or death. This pattern continued down the centuries and was seen at its most notorious in the conquest of the South American Indians by the conquistadores.

The crusades were another very dark chapter as the notion of Christendom developed — that is, the concept of an international Christian commonwealth of nations. That had been signalled in A. D. 800 when the pope crowned Charlemagne as the prototype Holy Roman Emperor. The aim of the crusades, which received full papal backing, was to wrest the so-called holy places in Palestine from the hands of the infidels. From a purely political point of view the movement ultimately failed. But from a spiritual standpoint it was an utter disaster, leaving us with the legacy of bitterness and suspicion in the Muslim world. It was all a far cry from the words of Jesus: 'My kingship is not of this world; if my kingship were of this world, my servants would fight' (John 18:36). Christians had forgotten the apostle Paul's words: 'For though we live in the world we are not carrying on a worldly war, for the weapons of our warfare are not worldly' (2 Cor. 10:3-4).

There was another ugly element in the developing situation. Discipline had always been seen as a necessary, if painful, factor in church life. Jesus had made it clear that the wilful sinner who refused to accept rebuke was to be excluded from the fellowship. Paul made the same point when he insisted that the blatantly immoral person was to be shut out of communion (Matt. 18:17; 1 Cor. 5:5). Now, however, in the sacral society an offence against the church was also a civil crime. While the church had always used moral persuasion and spiritual penalties, the state employed physical means, imprisonment, exile or death. The church's adoption of the state's methods began early, with exile being imposed, but it reached its ugly climax in A. D. 384 when Priscillian and his followers were put to death in spite of protests from many quarters, including the well-known Martin of Tours in Gaul.

There developed what can only be described as ecclesiastical hypocrisy. The term 'heresy' covered a wide range from outright denials of the faith to what people today would recognize as evangelical truth. The church would act as judge and impose the penalty. But because the church could not soil her hands with blood the condemned 'heretic' was handed over to the secular authorities, who in fact knew that if they failed to carry out the sentence they themselves would be in grave danger. The way forward had been mapped out. It would involve the horrors of the Spanish Inquisition and the final capitulation in England in A. D. 1302 with the promulgation of the edict on the burning of heretics. Tragically, the Protestant Reformers who grew up in the Roman Catholic system failed to recognize the falsity of the notion of the sacral society and sanctioned the persecution and the killing of Baptists — nicknamed Anabaptists or rebaptizers.

Pagan influences

Coming back to ordinary church life, we find that the secularizing of the church imported many ideas and practices which were pagan in origin and had no biblical warrant. One very popular cult at the time of Constantine and his successors was the veneration of the Mother Goddess. The cult had its roots in remote history but found new vigour in Egypt and the Mediterranean world. In Egypt Isis was pictured with her infant son Horus on her knee. Mary also began to be extolled, as the pagan Juno had been, as the protector of pregnant women. She was the guardian of cities, where she had the title 'Our Lady', a title she shared with the goddess Athena Polias. Isis, star of the sea *(Stella Maris)*, handed over her rôle as protector of sailors as well as her title. Churches dedicated to Mary occupied sites which were formerly the focus of pagan devotion.

Giovanni Miegge, the Waldensian scholar, illustrated this takeover of the pagan goddesses by pointing to churches in Rome itself: 'Santa Maria Antiqua, in Rome, stands in an area once consecrated to Pallas and before that again to the Etruscan

Minerva. Santa Maria in Aracoeli is built on the Capitoline hill where the celestial virgin — the Carthaginian Tanit — used to be worshipped... Santa Maria Maggiore, on the Esquiline, according to a medieval record was built on the site of a temple of Cybele, Mother of the Gods.'[1]

Turning to the weekly pattern of worship, when the believers met on the first day of the week to celebrate the resurrection of Jesus, it was in this area that the changing pattern of church life gradually became clearer. In pagan religions, which abounded like rank undergrowth in the fourth century, there was an animistic view of life in which the world was populated by good and evil spirits. The aim was to placate the threatening deities by sacrifices and to invoke the aid of benevolent deities. The sacrificing priests, with their altars of sacrifice, were central features in the cult.

The pattern of New Testament worship was starkly different. There was no such office as that of a priest, for every believer was a priest offering his or her body to the Lord (Rom. 12:1) or presenting 'a sacrifice of praise ... the fruit of lips that acknowledge his name' (Heb. 13:15). The pastor was essentially a preacher or teacher of the Word of God. The congregation gathered, not before an altar, but around a table which spoke, not of a propitiatory sacrifice, but of a family meal. The finality of Christ's one and only sacrifice was proclaimed in the visible word of the Lord's Supper, as it had been in the preaching of the Word. But now in the empire there was a major change. The pastor became the priest. The everyday clothes of the pastor gave way to special priestly garments. The table was replaced by a stone altar. The notion of a sacrifice being offered as a propitiation was established as the central act of worship for the new kind of adherents.

The ritual continued to develop. By A. D. 700-750 the priests' hands were anointed with oil. By around 750-780 the chasuble, the vestment worn over the white alb, was being

used as a priestly garment. The ninth century saw the speculation of Paschasius Radbertus that the bread in the eucharist
is the flesh born of Mary and is miraculously multiplied at each
consecration. In spite of the vigorous reply rejecting such a
theory penned by another monk, Ratramnus, Radbertus'
theory won the day. In 1215 the Fourth Lateran Council
formally declared the dogma of transubstantiation, the miraculous change of the bread and wine into the body and blood,
soul and divinity of Jesus Christ. In 1264 the feast of Corpus
Christi (Body of Christ) was established, with processions to
celebrate this mysterious change.

In so many areas of church life, what had begun as a
compromise with pagan teaching and practice became accepted policy. Thus when the pope Gregory the Great (A.D.
590-604) sent Augustine to England, he encouraged the
missionary to incorporate in his teaching and practice elements of existing pagan practice which he found useful. It is
not surprising that the old pagan shrines became centres of
pilgrimage. The old local deities re-emerged in the cult of the
saints when their shrines were furnished with relics of saints
and martyrs. It was the high road to syncretism, the fusion of
gospel and pagan elements. It is no wonder that an increasing
chasm yawned between the persecuted assemblies of Bible-
loving believers, the heirs of the early centuries, and the
worldly ecclesiastics, with their wealth and greed, who ruled
over a church which to any impartial observer seemed utterly
remote from the congregations of the Acts of the Apostles.

The rise of the papacy

Perhaps the most significant effect of the union of church and
state under Constantine and his successors was the increasing
prominence of the Bishop of Rome. In the New Testament

period a church would have a body of bishops or overseers. Thus Paul addressed his letter: 'To all the saints in Christ Jesus who are at Philippi, with the bishops and deacons' (Phil. 1:1). In his visit to Ephesus Paul speaks to the elders but also refers to them as 'overseers' — the word is literally bishops (Acts 20:28). So the pastors were designated as overseers and because of their standing they were called elders or presbyters. In other words, the terms 'elder' and 'bishop' were interchangeable.

As time went on one of the elders tended to become the leader, but he was still first among equals. However, the church of Rome, because of its location in the capital of the empire, became increasingly well known. The saying that all roads led to Rome was literally true, for the capital was the focal point of the marvellous road system of the empire. So the capital was constantly visited by a stream of visitors — soldiers, traders, government officials and representatives from the provinces or from lands beyond the empire. Like a twentieth-century church in London or Washington, the renown of a capital city gave the church and its leaders a widespread prominence.

The fall of Rome and the subsequent collapse of the Western empire thrust the Bishop of Rome into an even more prominent position. It was a time of chaos. A civilization was breaking up as the empire was divided among the warring tribes who entered into the old imperial heritage — the Lombards in Italy, the Franks in France, the Angles, Saxons and Jutes in England. In such times of social collapse people cling desperately to any institution which links them with a stable past which has disintegrated. The bishops of Rome filled that rôle as men and women recalled earlier years when the *pax Romana* had guaranteed social cohesion.

One of the most significant of these church leaders was Gregory, who was Bishop of Rome from A. D. 590-604. Born

into an upper-class Roman family, he was to many a living
embodiment of the old days of patrician influence. It is not
surprising that he spoke and acted with the old Roman confidence. It is one token of this assurance or arrogance that the
title *'Pappa'* (father) was reserved as a title for the Bishop of
Rome.

The claims of his successors mounted. The crowning of
Charlemagne emphasized the dependence of the empire on the
church. Around A. D. 837 Gregory IV issued the legendary
account of the Donation of Constantine. This totally spurious
story recalled the alleged bestowal on the pope by Constantine
of authority over Italy and the west of Europe. This legend was
exposed as spurious by the Renaissance scholar Laurentius
Valla in 1440. At the same time Valla exposed as a forgery the
pseudo-Isadorian decretals. Attributed to Isadore of Seville,
who died in A.D. 636, and alleged to be the letters and decrees
of the popes, these decretals were in fact issued by Pope
Nicholas I in the ninth century. They have been the foundation
of so many of the subsequent papal claims. Although Catholic
scholars today would accept the Renaissance exposure of the
forgeries they seem perfectly content to retain the edifice of
papal claims built on these documents even though the foundation has been removed.

Popes and emperors continued an ongoing struggle as one
side tried to claim primacy over the other. In fact they became
like two competing rulers and were not always too worried by
the tactics they employed. Henry II of England was glad to
have the blessing of Adrian IV, the only English pope, for his
invasion of Ireland, but after his clash with the church which
led to the murder of Thomas à Beckett, Archbishop of Canterbury, he had to do penance for his sins!

The rise of the national states led to frequent tension
between kings and popes. It was in response to such pressure
that Boniface VIII in 1302 issued the famous bull (the word

was derived from the Latin word *bulla*, the seal on the document) *Extra Ecclesiam nulla salus* ('Outside the church there is no salvation'). He asserted his sovereign rights over the rulers of the world and insisted that for anyone to be saved it was necessary that they should be subject to the Roman pontiff.

Dark years for the papacy

The decline in papal power over the rulers of Europe was greatly increased by political involvement. When the papacy moved from Rome to Avignon in France the popes were subject to the influence of the French king. An abortive return to Rome led to a schism when one pope reigned in Rome and another in Avignon. The nations of Europe were divided. The kings of England involved in the Hundred Years' War with France did not take kindly to French influence. Others took sides and popes hurled anathemas against their rivals. Finally the Council of Pisa in 1409 rejected both popes and elected Alexander V, but still the schism continued. John XXIII succeeded Alexander but was himself deposed by the Council of Constance in 1415. So the ludicrous situation had gone on for forty years when the claimed necessity of having a visible head of the church of Christ clashed with farcical competition to be acclaimed as the genuine article.

The popes had become worldly princes who had their own papal states in central Italy. The picture of Julius II in full armour leading the attack on Bologna was totally incompatible with his claims to be Christ's representative. But worldliness and blatant immorality were not a new phenomenon in the history of the papacy. The Renaissance popes had forerunners. The ninth, tenth and eleventh centuries were particularly notorious. The record of lust, fornication, cruelty, greed and murder is so appalling that were it not for solid historical evidence it might be viewed as a scurrilous invention of anti-papal writers. Sadly the record is only too well substantiated.

In the eighth century, when Paul I died, a soldier called Constantine was hurriedly ordained and made pope. He lasted over a year until Stephen III ousted him and had his eyes torn out — a favourite Roman penalty at that time! Even if Stephen was not personally involved in that, he was involved directly in the blinding and killing of others. The tenth and eleventh centuries plumbed ever greater depths of iniquity. Notorious women were closely involved in the moral chaos. Marozia, well known as a prostitute, had a son by Pope Sergius III, whom the Roman Catholic historian Duchesne described as 'spiteful, brutal and a scoundrel'.[2] That son was later to become pope as John XI, who was infamous for his vileness. John XII was no better. Duchesne wrote, 'His illicit amours were a matter of public knowledge, for they were restrained neither by ties of blood nor of respect.'

Worse was to follow with such men as Benedict IX, who earned the reputation of being possibly the worst pope who ever lived. He was only twelve when he became pope and lived a life of utter debauchery with adulteries and murders as his achievements. It was not a Protestant but a Roman Catholic cardinal, Baronius, who asked the searching question: 'What was then the aspect of the Holy Roman Church? How utterly foul when harlots most powerful and most vile dominated Rome; at whose will sees were changed, bishops presented — and, what is horrible to hear, and unspeakable — their lovers intruded into the see of Peter.'[3]

The popes in Avignon in the fourteenth century were notorious for their corruption and general depravity. The schism divided Avignon and Roman popes but there was little or nothing to choose between them in terms of immorality and ruthlessness. Urban VI was so vile that a plea of insanity was made in an attempt to whitewash the horror of it all.

The fifteenth century, with the popes back in Rome, showed little change. There was a succession of deeply evil men whose corruption not only brought the papacy into disrepute but affected moral standards across Italy. Typical was Innocent VIII, who fathered many children, celebrated at the Vatican the marriages of his dissolute son and of two of his granddaughters. It all led up to the climax of Alexander VI, who broke all the records for corruption and immorality. He bribed his way to win election as pope. His children received favoured treatment. The notorious Lucretia Borgia, who was his daughter, had both her marriages celebrated in the Vatican. She was even appointed by her father to deputize for him when he was absent from Rome, and so she presided over the meeting of the cardinals. One of his sons was made a cardinal and later became Paul III. Alexander's record was appalling, yet this was the pope under whose authority Savonarola, the great Dominican preacher, was brutally killed after he rejected the ecclesiastical ban imposed by Alexander, whom Savonarola described as a representative of Satan, not of God.

The question of papal authority

I can hear someone saying, 'Why dip into these murky depths?' Certainly I agree that all this does not provide very edifying reading. However it is a very useful corrective to the grandiose claims made by Rome for the papacy. If there were a few moral lapses they might conceivably be explained away. But here — and I have only touched the edge of the subject — you have long periods of degeneracy spread over several centuries. We are entitled to ask, 'Were these the "holy fathers"?' The very word 'holy' simply does not remotely fit into the seemingly unending history of iniquity and blatant sensuality. It will not do to plead that the Counter-Reformation set new standards and the popes who followed were very far removed from the Borgia pope. Surely we cannot allow this easy dismissal of whole generations of men and women who were subject to papal teaching and guidance, when in fact the popes were blind guides and often ruthless exploiters of their people.

The claim is frequently made that the dogma of papal infallibility was not a novelty enacted in 1870 at the First Vatican Council. The council, so it is asserted, simply stated in a clear and explicit way the teaching that had always been a reality in the life of the church. So we are expected to accept that a long line of debauched men whose villainy is the despair of many Roman Catholic historians were in fact the infallible guides necessary to guide the church.

There is an even more important factor which makes the sordid record so significant. It is the nature of the sacraments, which in Roman teaching are the ways in which God's grace flows to us. Now, for a sacrament to be valid there are very specific requirements. There must be the right matter — water in baptism and bread and wine in the Lord's Supper. There must be the right form — namely, the invocation of the Trinity in baptism and the words of consecration in the eucharist. But there is a further essential requirement if a sacrament is to be valid — the celebrant must have the right intention. He must, in other words, intend to do what the church requires. He must carry out the intentions of the church concerning the celebration of the sacrament. Without that intention the sacrament is void.

Now Rome teaches that ordination is a sacrament. The intention is that the man being ordained priest shall be authorized and equipped with power to offer the sacrifice of the mass. Indeed the absence of the right intention was one of the reasons given in the papal bull of Leo XIII in 1896, the *Apostolicæ Curæ*, which declared Anglican orders null and void. Yet we are asked to accept that the cynical blackguards who in great numbers disgraced their office had the right intention in the masses they said, the marriages they performed and the ordinations they carried out. That really would be to stretch credulity far beyond breaking-point. Yet every invalid sacrament, especially every invalid ordination, meant one more break in the so-called apostolic succession. Indeed, it casts a shadow even on popes of moral integrity, whose record stands out in stark contrast with the shameful saga of many others. How could honourable men like Celestine I or Paul II be sure that the cardinals who laid hands on them, or indeed the bishops who ordained them, had the right intention?

If the Council of Trent and the Counter-Reformation dealt with some of the grosser forms of papal iniquity they in no way diminished papal authority. That authority had been asserted with a steadily increasing arrogance. Back in the eleventh century Gregory VII (Hildebrand) felt himself strong enough to excommunicate the emperor and to keep him standing in the snow at Canossa awaiting the papal pardon. King John of England faced the same assertion of papal authority and had to capitulate and accept the papal nominee to the archbishopric of Canterbury. When therefore Boniface VIII made his grandiose claims to universal dominion he was simply building on his predecessor's policies and on the forgeries which they all gladly accepted.

Such was the overwhelming confidence of the popes in their boastful claims that both Leo X and his successor Clement VII failed to appreciate the significance of Martin Luther. To them he was an obscure German monk who could easily be dealt with. In any case they were too involved in political intrigues to remove the emperor. The latter incidentally had the last laugh as his troops pillaged Rome.

Another major threat to papal pretensions came with the French Revolution, followed by the dictatorship of Napoleon. Pius VI died in a French prison. His successor, Pius VII, fared no better. In spite of his sharing in the crowning of Napoleon as emperor in 1804 the suspicion that the pope was conspiring with France's enemies led to his arrest and the confiscation of the papal states. It seemed as if the papacy was finished. In fact it was Napoleon who ended his days as a prisoner on St Helena. At the Congress of Vienna, which the victorious allies convened to resettle Europe, the papal states were restored and the wealth which had been commandeered by the French was given back. The papal states were notorious for abuse of civil rights and simmering discontent was simply a long-drawn-out prelude to their final conquest by Garibaldi in his campaign for the unification of Italy. The victory of the Italian nationalist brought the First Vatican Council to a premature end and led to the papacy becoming confined to the Vatican. This was due to papal policy which only changed when the Vatican signed a concordat, or agreement, with the fascist dictator Mussolini in 1929.

The main issue of the council was, however, secured — namely the definition, as a binding dogma, of the infallibility of the pope. There was strong opposition from the members of the council with one of the most trenchant rejections coming from Bishop Josef Strossmayer.[4] He was one of over a hundred bishops who initially voted against the proposed dogma. There were many other very powerful voices in the opposition, such as Hefele the historian and Von Dollinger, both of whom had a European-wide reputation for scholarship. The arm-twisting was intense. Many bishops felt they could not face a public vote against the pope. Their only answer was to leave the council before its adjournment with the shadow of Garibaldi's men approaching. The result was really a manipulated verdict.

The dogma defined the issue firmly. When the pope speaks ex *cathedra*, that is, from his throne, as pastor of the universal church, and when he defines a dogma concerning faith and morals, it is binding on all Christians and is not subject to modification by any church council.

The pope appealed to tradition and to history. The claim was made, and is still maintained, that the council simply stated in explicit terms what had always been taught. Any unbiased historian would soon demolish such pretensions. One might point to the Arian controversy in the fourth century. The crucial issue was the person of Christ — was he truly 'of one substance with the Father'? Arius rejected this and the courageous Bishop of Alexandria seemed to belong to a tiny minority — it was *'Athanasius contra mundum'* (Athanasius against the world). Pope Liberius sided with Arius and excommunicated Athanasius. The best verdict on the pope was given by Hilary of Poitiers, the Athanasius of the west: 'I say anathema to thee, Liberius, and to thy accomplices.' Ironically Hilary was proclaimed a Doctor of the Church by Pius IX, the author of the claim to papal infallibility!

Pius IX, however, also blundered over the issue of Philomena. Tradition had long given an exalted place to this third-century martyr. She had been proclaimed a saint by Pope Leo XII. Pius IX encouraged the cult and appointed a mass in her honour. The only basis for the story of Philomena was a dream by a nun in which she had a 'revelation' about the holy virgin martyred under the Emperor Diocletian. Sadly for all those who were devoted to her and all those who had been given her name, Roman Catholic scholars were finally compelled to acknowledge that there never was such a person as Philomena. So the 'infallible guides' had been encouraging people for years to invoke a figment of someone's imagination. Their dismissal of many of the alleged saints was well summed up in one newspaper headline at the time: 'When the saints go marching out.' Interestingly the fallible Irish scholar George Salmon, over a century ago in his lectures in the divinity school of Dublin University, totally rejected the legend. He gave his lectures in 1870 — if only Pius IX had attended them!

Returning to the record of the early centuries we find further examples of evidently fallible bishops of Rome. In the fifth century Zosimus pronounced the arch-heretic Pelagius 'impeccably orthodox'. Later the infallible guide withdrew his very fallible decision. In the next century Vigilius acted like the famous vicar of Bray in the song who altered his views to suit 'whatever king may reign'. In the debate over the relationship between the two natures in the person of Christ, he embraced first one erroneous extreme and then another, and finally accepted the orthodox faith in face of his condemnation by the Council of Constantinople.

Coming to more modern times, we find the massive blunders of Sixtus V (1585-1590). He issued a standard version of the Vulgate — the Latin translation of the Bible. This was for centuries the one Bible accepted in Rome. This acceptance led to the rejection of translations into the vernacular. Sixtus made it clear that this was not simply a scholarly issue but one that involved papal authority. So he wrote his preface with the kind of authority Pius IX claimed in 1870: 'By the fulness of Apostolic power we decree and declare that this edition approved by the authority delivered to us by the Lord, is to be received and held as true, lawful, authentic and unquestioned in all public and private discussion, reading, preaching and explanations.' The trouble for Sixtus was that the scholars displayed a catalogue of mistakes he had made. His successor had to produce a new edition in which the fallible scholars did a much better job than the infallible editor had done!

One of the most sordid examples of this exercise of papal power was the matter of Galileo, the great pioneer, together with Copernicus, of modern astronomy. He clashed with Rome. The ecclesiastical orthodoxy rejected the claim of both these men that the earth went round the sun. Galileo faced the

Inquisition and was forced to deny what he knew to be the truth. His subsequent writing showed that he still maintained what every schoolchild today knows as fact. He was brought before Urban VIII. Facing the threat of torture and in face of his weakness — he was ill and nearly seventy — he was forced to capitulate. The works of Copernicus and Galileo remained on the list of forbidden books until 1831 when, to quote W. S. Kerr's ironic comment, 'The earth received papal permission to move.'[5]

The need today

So we come to the present time near the end of the twentieth century. It is almost seventeen centuries since Constantine fought the battle of the Milvian bridge and the long compromise between church and state began. It was a compromise which became so embedded in men's minds that even the Reformation failed to deal with it. So Martin Luther made his appeal to the German princes. Whether in Calvin's Geneva, John Knox's Scotland, or the England of Elizabeth, the notion of an intimate church/state relationship continued. In Protestantism the witness and suffering of the Anabaptists and the rise of religious nonconformity challenged the old notion of established churches. But the papacy remained wedded to that policy and even in lands where Roman Catholicism was a minority there was the panoply of an international body with its papal nuncios or legates acting like foreign ministers of an imperial power.

Malachi Martin, formerly professor in the pontifical biblical institute in Rome, summed up the situation as he recalled the long history since Silvester I collaborated with Constantine to launch the new order of things. He wrote, 'Since the time of Silvester I ... the history of Christianity is one in which its spiritual message has either been muffled in ermine or skewered by its own golden sword.'[6] The answer surely is clear. What is needed is a return to Jesus' original pattern for the church: 'My kingship is not of this world' (John 18:36). The apostle Paul has the same message: 'Though we live in the world we are not carrying on a worldly war' (2 Cor. 10:3). The final victory, according to John, will be 'by the blood of the Lamb and by the word of their testimony' (Rev. 12:11).

3.
Scripture and tradition

When someone is taking the first, perhaps rather tentative, steps towards faith he or she is usually full of questions: 'What is God like? What does God require from me? What did Jesus Christ accomplish when he died?' The Christian friend or pastor who is helping the enquirer points to the Bible. Here is where the message of Christ is to be found. Here are the demands of God for repentance and faith. Here is the pattern of Christian living. So right from the outset the emphasis is on discovering what the Bible has to say.

When that enquirer becomes a believer, is baptized and moves into the fellowship of a local church the same emphasis continues. When the preacher is speaking in the service of worship on the Lord's day he is, or should be, endeavouring to open up the text for the hearers to understand and also, very importantly, to apply. When the notices are given out mention may be made of house groups where Christians will meet to study the Bible. The new believer finds as well that there is great encouragement to engage in personal daily Bible study. The whole emphasis is on the importance of the Bible as God's Word to us.

This attitude lay at the heart of the great spiritual awakening in the sixteenth century. Martin Luther, an Augustinian monk and a professor of theology, had tried everywhere to find an answer to the most basic of all spiritual questions: 'How may

I, as a sinner, stand before a holy God and be accepted?' It was when he endeavoured to explain to his students Paul's letter to the Romans that the light dawned in his own soul. It is no wonder that he came to the conclusion that God speaks to humble seekers after truth through the Scriptures.

Luther had taught the tradition of the church for years. He had tried to discover the answer in the teachings of the scholastic philosophers. He wanted desperately to remain an obedient servant of the Roman Catholic Church. Yet he found himself driven by the ecclesiastical leaders to discover that it was not in their accumulated traditions, but in the Scriptures, that he would hear God's voice. Facing his accusers at the gathering of German princes at Worms, he was called on to retract his teaching on purgatory and indulgences. In reply he made his famous defence: 'Unless I am convicted by Scripture and plain reason — I do not accept the authorities of popes and councils, for they have contradicted each other — my conscience is captive to the Word of God. I cannot and I will not recant anything for to go against conscience is neither right nor safe.' This refusal to accept any other authority above or alongside Scripture was to become the driving force of the Reformation. The slogan *'Sola Scriptura'* (Scripture alone) was not a theory born of speculation. It was a conviction hammered out on the anvil of a man's soul.

The latter half of the twentieth century has seen a remarkable change in the attitude to Scripture among Roman Catholics. I can recall a time when the Bible was largely the prerogative of the priests. For most people it was a book which they were discouraged from reading. Indeed the old-fashioned traditionalists were still arguing that it required the trained mind of the priest to understand. Personal Bible study could open the way to querying the teaching of the Catholic Church. As events proved they were correct in their judgement. Today, when it is normal for Catholics to read their Bibles and when

Bible study groups are common, there has been a great deal of radical thinking and it has led very many out of Rome.

The traditional Catholic position

What has gone wrong, from a Roman Catholic point of view, is that there has been an underlying failure to understand what is of fundamental importance — namely, that the Bible by itself is insufficient, if not indeed spiritually dangerous. The Council of Trent, for whom Luther was a heretic, formulated a notion as far removed as possible from *'Sola Scriptura'*. In its fourth session it made clear that it accepted a twofold source of truth: Scripture and tradition. 'It [the Council] receives and venerates with the same sense of loyalty and reverence all the books of the Old and New Testament, for God alone is the author of both — together with all the traditions concerning faith and morals, as coming from the mouth of Christ or being inspired by the Holy Spirit and preserved in continuous succession in the Catholic Church.'[1] In article 215 there is a significant addition which reinforces this qualifying of Scripture: 'It belongs to her [the Church] to judge the true meaning of Scripture — and that no one dare to interpret the Scripture in a way contrary to the unanimous consensus of the Fathers even though such interpretations be not intended for publication.'[2]

The First Vatican Council underlined the teaching of Trent. It is not surprising that it did so, for the chief item on the agenda of the council was the new theory, challenged by many of the council members, that the pope speaking as pastor of the universal church is infallible in his teaching. They would certainly have needed tradition for that idea, for Scripture would be totally against it! So they decreed in Chapter III: 'All those things are to be believed with divine and Catholic faith which are contained in the Word of God written or handed down and which by the Church, either in solemn judgement or through her ordinary and universal teaching office, are proposed for belief as having been divinely revealed.'[3]

The Second Vatican Council was hailed by many as the great renewal council which changed the whole direction of the Roman Catholic Church. Yet it is as firm as Trent or Vatican I on this issue of Scripture and tradition. 'Therefore both Scripture and Tradition should be accepted with equal sentiments of devotion and reverence... Sacred Tradition and Holy Scripture form a single sacred deposit of the Word of God entrusted to the Church.'[4]

There is an even clearer assertion of the third factor in the situation, namely the magisterium — that is, the teaching office in the church: 'It is clear therefore that sacred Tradition, Holy Scripture and the Church's magisterium are by God's most wise decree so closely connected and associated together that one does not subsist without the other two, and that all of them, and each in its own manner, under the impulse of the one Spirit of God, contribute efficaciously to the salvation of souls.'[5] Lest the point should be missed that the teaching authority of the church is a vital element, the decree on the pastoral office of bishops takes the same line. 'Their teaching', it is claimed, 'is based on sacred Scripture, tradition, the liturgy, the teaching authority, and life of the Church.'[6]

Some may try to counter all this evidence of Catholic views on Scripture by quoting the new attitude in renewal circles and among those who call themselves evangelical Catholics. It should be noted therefore that the new Vatican Catechism is firmly in support of the traditional position. The claim is made that 'The Church to whom the transmission and interpretation of Revelation is entrusted does not derive her certainty about all revealed truths from the Holy Scriptures alone. Both Scripture and Tradition must be accepted and honoured with equal sentiments of devotion and reverence.'[7]

Jesus and the Pharisees

This matter of Scripture and tradition did not emerge as a new controversy in the sixteenth century. It was a live issue in the days of Jesus. Again and again he encountered the appeal of the Pharisees to their traditions. Of course, they wholeheartedly accepted the Scriptures of the Old Testament as the Word of God to which they must submit. They recognized the threefold division into the Law, the Prophets and the Writings, but that recognition in no way modified or negated acceptance of the unity of the Old Testament. Yet at the same time they would make their appeal to the traditions which they had received from their fathers and which, for them, were also authoritative. The great rabbinic teachers had commented on the Scriptures and had endeavoured to apply their teaching to the pattern of worship and to the daily lives of their people. This mass of writings and the developed norms of conduct had an authority which stood alongside that of the Scriptures and at times qualified, or even violated, the law.

Jesus never presented himself as the inaugurator of a new religion. He had a profound reverence for the Old Testament Scriptures, which he frequently quoted and to which he ascribed an unassailable pre-eminence. In the same way his disciples saw themselves as the spiritual heirs of Abraham. They were not innovators but rather devout Israelites who were privileged to be disciples of Jesus of Nazareth, whom they came to recognize as the Messiah. Hence to look at the issue of tradition in relation to the Old Testament is not some academic exercise with largely antiquarian interest. Rather it demonstrates the unique primacy of Scripture and helps us to meet the same conflict between Scripture and tradition as it affects the New Testament.

What made — and continues to make — the matter so serious was that tradition not only competed with Scripture but again and again substituted for it the teaching of men, and claimed for such teaching the authority which belongs to the Word of God. The Pharisees could see the issue clearly. That is why they challenged Jesus: 'Why do your disciples not live according to the tradition of the elders?' (Mark 7:5; Matt. 15:2). Jesus rejected their challenge out of hand. What they were doing, he said, was 'teaching as doctrines the precepts of men' (Matt. 15:9; Mark 7:7). Worse still, they not only elevated 'the tradition of the elders' to the level of Scripture, but by that very elevation they were 'making void the word of God' through their traditions. Jesus pressed the point. Their adherence to their traditions meant that they transgressed the commandment of God, even as they accused the disciples of transgressing the tradition of the elders (Matt. 15:2-3). He went further in his counter-charge, declaring, 'So for the sake of your tradition, you have made void the Word of God' (Matt. 15:6; Mark 7:13).

In Matthew 23 there is an extended treatment of the guilt which Jesus laid at the door of the religious leaders. Their readiness to let the traditions of the elders qualify the Scriptures had led them into hypocrisy — the word means literally 'play-acting' and their theories had led them to play an elaborate rôle which was endorsed by their traditions but condemned by Scriptures. So their traditions had led to elaborate ritual, eye-catching vestments and venerable ecclesiastical titles. They enjoyed being called 'rabbi' by men but that, said Jesus, was totally wrong. 'You are not to be called rabbi, for you have one teacher, and you are all brethren. And call no man your father on earth, for you have one Father, who is in heaven' (Matt. 23:8-9). Then followed a long list of awesome denunciations in all of which we see the competing traditions of the elders utterly rejected by Christ and the Scriptures being declared to be the sole criterion of revealed truth.

The testimony of the New Testament writers

The disciples learnt the lesson well. So it is no surprise, when we come to the New Testament writings, to find the same relegation to a secondary position of human tradition. The constant refrain is their subjection to the supreme authority of the Scriptures. The New Testament was essentially the permanent embodiment in written form of the apostolic testimony. When Jesus called twelve men, it was with a view to their being eyewitnesses of his ministry and especially of his resurrection. Those aims were spelled out precisely (Acts 1:21-22) when Matthias was elected to take the place of the apostate Judas Iscariot. The apostle Paul was appointed to this select group of eyewitnesses as the risen Christ met him on the Damascus road. Thus he, with them, was authorized to pass on the apostolic testimony.

As eyewitnesses of the risen Christ, the apostles were a unique body. Since it would be impossible for any subsequent generation to experience the Lord's resurrection at first hand, it would be equally impossible for them to have any successors. There would be in the centuries ahead a great number of preachers and writers who would endeavour to apply the apostolic testimony to their own generation and to the problems emerging in their own culture. Yet they would never have the immediacy of the once-for-all experience of personal witnesses. That is why Christians in the long history ahead would not only affirm again and again the uniqueness of the New Testament, but would discover, by the powerful enlightenment of the Holy Spirit, that the Scriptures were not a far-distant testimony requiring to be supplemented by subsequent wisdom. Those Scriptures would be so written in the hearts of readers that by the Spirit's illumination they would come with the freshness with which they came to the earliest believers.

Within the New Testament there is so much evidence of the supreme authority of the Scriptures. The four Gospels have a constant refrain: '... that the Scriptures might be fulfilled'. The virgin birth of Jesus, his sinless life, his atoning death and his glorious resurrection — all are seen as fulfilment of the Old Testament Scriptures. So in his record of Paul's ministry Luke makes a specially favourable reference to the men of Berea because 'They received the word with all eagerness, examining the scriptures daily to see if these things were so' (Acts 17:11).

The apostolic preaching recorded in Acts and the careful doctrinal arguments in the epistles are constantly reinforced by appeal to quotations from the Scriptures. There is a clear assumption by preachers and writers that their hearers would share their own recognition of the supremacy of the written Word. Where there were godly families there would already be ripe ground for sowing the seed of the gospel. So Paul reminded Timothy of the privilege of having a godly mother and grandmother so that 'From childhood you have been acquainted with the sacred writings which are able to instruct you for salvation through faith in Christ Jesus' (2 Tim. 3:15).

The powerful impact upon the minds and hearts of the biblical writers was the action of the Holy Spirit. So when Paul continues with his message to Timothy he writes, 'All scripture is inspired by God.' The Greek word means literally 'God-breathed'. We use that kind of phraseology when we share a special secret with a friend and add: 'Don't breathe a word!' To breathe a word is to utter a word. So Paul is claiming that beyond the authors of the Scriptures there is the divine Author giving us the 'God-breathed' Word.

The apostle Peter has the same emphasis: 'No prophecy ever came by the impulse of man, but men moved by the Holy Spirit spoke from God' (2 Peter 1:21). The Greek word translated 'moved' is a graphic one. It would have been used in Greek shipping circles of a ship with a favourable following breeze being borne along by the wind. So the biblical authors were powerfully impelled by the breath of God.

Someone may query the whole drift of my argument, and point out that the references quoted in the New Testament refer only to the Old. By way of reply it is worth noting that the New Testament writings did not drop from heaven as a single book but were written over quite a number of years. Hence the testimony as to their acceptance as being on a level with the Old Testament is implicit in the text rather than being spelled out in precise detail. However, we still have clear indications of this kind of testimony to the authority of New Testament writings. Thus in this same second letter of Peter, he refers to the writings of Paul. He acknowledges that some of them are hard to grasp — it is good to realize that our struggle to elucidate some of the details of Romans or 2 Corinthians were shared by Peter! Of much greater significance is the fact that he puts Paul's letters on the same level as 'the other scriptures' (2 Peter 3:16), and earlier, as we have seen, he meant by 'Scripture' the Word given by God.

The epistle to the Hebrews has the same emphasis. The argument of this letter is that the prophecies, symbolism and priesthood of the Old Testament have found their fulfilment in Jesus Christ. This means that the New Testament comes from the same God who moved Moses and the prophets to write their great prophetic statement of what was yet to be fulfilled. So the letter to the Hebrews begins with an insistence that the God whose Word was spoken in and through the Old Testament has spoken with a like authority in the New. So the epistle begins with one of the most majestic statements in the Bible: 'In many and various ways God spoke of old to our fathers by the prophets; but in these last days he has spoken to us by a Son.'

The same recognition of the supreme authority of the apostolic testimony emerges sometimes in incidental references. So, after Paul's long discussion on tongues and prophecy, and his direction as to how such utterances should be controlled,

he adds a firm and authoritative comment: 'If anyone thinks he
is a prophet, or spiritual, he should acknowledge that what I am
writing to you is a command of the Lord. If anyone does not
recognize this he is not recognized' (1 Cor. 14:37-38).

'A full and perfect rule of faith'

Does the ultimate revelation of divine truth have a twofold
origin in Scripture and tradition? Are both to be held in equal
reverence? The answer I have suggested to that question is to
be found in the Scriptures themselves which have a unique rôle
as the utterance of the Most High God. One might add a wry
comment by George Salmon, penned over a century ago. He
was arguing for the supreme authority of Scripture, so one can
sense the underlying humour in his remark: 'We might be well
content to allow the question concerning Scripture and tradition to be determined by tradition alone; for if anything can be
established by tradition, there is a full and clear tradition to
prove that the Scriptures are a full and perfect rule of faith; that
they contain the whole Word of God; and that what is outside
them need not be regarded.'[8]

He also drew a practical lesson as he pointed to the contrast
between a compact Bible and the vast library of tradition. If the
latter is to be equated with the writings of the theologians, the
encyclicals of the popes and the ongoing understanding of the
church, then one is talking about an enormous range of
writings which it would take the keenest of scholars a few
lifetimes to study. To say by way of reply that this indicates the
necessity of the magesterium to discern what are the true
traditions is to raise the issue which Vatican II presented as its
conclusion — namely, that Scripture and tradition alike require the teaching office within the church. So to that issue we
must turn in the next chapter.

4.
Infallible?

It seems to be a continuing human reaction to the status of leadership to devise titles to stress the importance of the person so designated. So we get 'His Excellency', 'His Majesty', 'His Imperial Majesty', etc. The churches have tended to respond in a similar fashion with a graded series from 'Reverend' to 'Very...', 'Right...' and 'Most Reverend'. It should not surprise us, then, to find the Bishop of Rome displaying his claimed pre-eminence in the titles he bears. These titles are not, however, like those in other ecclesiastical usages — mere pretentious adornment — for in fact they embody the enormous claims of the papacy to play a key rôle in the work of salvation.

The pope's titles

The 'Holy Father'

Take the title 'the Holy Father'. This certainly is a biblical title. It was used by none other than the Son of God himself. It was uttered on a particularly solemn occasion. Jesus was about to take leave of his disciples and face the betrayal by Judas, denial by Peter, rejection by his own people and death at the hands of the Romans. Such a prayer, with the shadows of the cross so evident, made the occasion singularly moving as the Saviour prayed for his disciples and for those in the future who would share their faith. So he prays: 'Holy Father, keep them in thy name' (John 17:11).

It is abundantly clear that the title belongs uniquely to the Lord God Almighty. It was not applied to any apostle. The apostles would have been horrified if someone had transferred to them the honour that belonged to God alone. Had they been tempted — though this is a fanciful thought — to assume the title they must surely have remembered Jesus' cautionary word: 'Call no man your father on earth, for you have one Father, who is in heaven' (Matt. 23:9). Of this heavenly Father Jesus spoke often, and the various words he used to accompany the title were 'perfect', 'holy' and 'righteous'. It beggars imagination that any mortal and sinful man should dare to take the title of the God of glory and use it to designate himself.

The 'Supreme Pontiff'

Then there is the title 'Supreme Pontiff'. It is still very much in evidence. Indeed, it appears in the papal introduction to the Vatican Catechism which John Paul dates as '11th October 1992 ... in the fourteenth year of my Pontificate'. The word 'pontiff' is derived from the Latin word *pontifex*, which itself is a combination of two other Latin words: *facio* (I make) and *pons* (a bridge). So the word 'pontiff' means 'bridge builder'. It had been used in the imperial cult in Rome where the priest, as is customary in any pagan religion, offered the sacrifices in order to placate the deity and so provide access to the divine favour — hence the title 'bridge builder'. In the practice of the cult of the emperor in Rome there were a number of priests, with one presiding over them who was designated the supreme pontiff. So the title is redolent of the paganism from which it came.

When the gospel broke with power into the Roman world it brought a new notion of priesthood. Jesus Christ, the apostles preached, was sent by God to be the anointed Prophet, Priest and King. As priest he was unique in that he was both priest and victim, since the sacrifice he offered was himself. He was 'the Lamb of God who takes away the sin of the world!' (John 1:29). His altar was the cross of Calvary. His resurrection and ascension were the divine authentication of his priestly offering. He is thus the unique High Priest.

The letter to the Hebrews stresses that his priesthood was not only the exposure of the emptiness of all pagan priestly activity, but it also eclipsed the priesthood of the Old Testament by fulfilling the purposes for which the Levites had been set apart. Alongside the inadequacy of their sacrifices, which could never take away sin (Heb. 10:4), there stood his one perfect sacrifice which would never be repeated. Alongside the faded glory of the Levitical priesthood the letter to the Hebrews highlights the stark contrast: 'And every priest stands daily at his service, offering repeatedly the same sacrifices, which can never take away sins. But when Christ had offered for all time a single sacrifice for sins, he sat down at the right hand of God' (Heb. 10: 11-12).

Here, in all the splendour of his priestly ministry, is Jesus the Supreme Pontiff. That title is his, and his alone. The apostles Paul and Peter, so prominent among the apostles, would have uttered a ringing anathema on anyone who dared to usurp the title, and so the glory, of our heavenly High Priest.

The 'Vicar of Christ'

We turn to another frequently used title, 'the Vicar of Christ'. The Latin word *vicarius* means 'one who takes another's place, a substitute'. We are not left to speculate as to the person to whom that title belongs, for Jesus himself made it very clear that the one who took his place was the Holy Spirit. This was disclosed to his disciples as he comforted them in view of his impending death and his subsequent return to glory. He knew that the prospect of being left on their own was quite devastating. How would they cope in a hostile world without his reassuring presence? There was so much that they still had to learn. Who would teach them when he had gone?

The answer to these questions was a series of promises that he would send someone to take his place: 'I will pray the Father, and he will give you another Counsellor, to be with you for ever... I will not leave you desolate ... the Counsellor, the Holy Spirit, whom the Father will send in my name, he will teach you all things... When the Counsellor comes, whom I shall send to you from the Father, even the Spirit of truth, who proceeds from the Father...' (John 14:16,18,26; 15:26). All this is echoed in the creed of Nicæa as it speaks of the Spirit, 'who proceedeth from the Father and the Son, who with the Father and the Son together is worshipped and glorified'.

So the papal titles are not simply somewhat grandiose designations which have evolved in the course of Christian history. They are rather a very grave usurpation of the titles of the Godhead. We bow and worship the Holy Father, our Creator, Lord and Judge. We come through the sole mediatorship of our Lord Jesus Christ, the Supreme Pontiff, the great High Priest (Heb. 4:15). We rejoice in the indwelling presence of the Holy Spirit, the Vicar of Christ, who makes the presence of the heavenly Christ a deep reality in our own experience. To take on our lips these great titles is to tread on holy ground as we are in the presence not of a man, but of the triune God.

We have already seen, in chapter 2, the way the office of the Bishop of Rome became transformed into a universal jurisdiction. But at this point it is necessary to examine the biblical evidence which Rome uses to justify its enormous claims for papal supremacy. It is a far cry from the presiding overseer in the congregation in Rome to which the apostle Paul sent his epistle, to one who claims to rule over the worldwide churches of Christ.

'Upon this rock' (Matt. 16:13-19)

The most obvious starting-point is Matthew 16:18-19, which has been often quoted as the charter for all subsequent claims. It was the reply Jesus gave to Peter's affirmation that Jesus is the Messiah, the Son of the living God: 'I tell you, you are Peter, and on this rock I will build my church, and the powers of death shall not prevail against it.' The notes appended to the Catholic edition of the Revised Standard Version give the traditional explanation: 'The name "Peter" comes from the Greek word for "rock". Jesus makes him the foundation on which the church is to be built.' The Vatican Catechism takes the same line, claiming that 'The Lord made Simon whom he named Peter the "rock" of his Church.'[1] The catechism goes further and designates him as 'the Pope, Bishop of Rome and Peter's successor'. It has more to add: 'The Roman Pontiff by reason of his office as Vicar of Christ, and as pastor of the entire church has full, supreme and universal power over the whole Church, a power which he can always exercise unhindered.'

Before examining the main issue, namely the meaning of the rock, we must ask some preliminary questions to each of which the answer is surely an emphatic 'No'! Does this verse give Peter primacy over the other apostles? Does the verse declare Peter's infallibility? Can you find here any reference to Peter's successors? Could an eyewitness of the resurrection have any successors? Does the verse — or indeed any verse in the New Testament — identify Peter with the Bishop of Rome?

Was Peter Bishop of Rome?

To deal with the last question first, one may examine the New
Testament for evidence of Peter as Bishop of Rome, but there
is a stunning silence. Paul wrote his letter to Rome but in
greeting various members of the church there he makes no
mention of Peter. Perhaps he had not yet emerged, hence the
silence! But much later, when Paul arrived in Rome, there was
a welcome from the brethren but still no sign of Peter. When
Paul, much later still, wrote his prison epistles from Rome to
believers in Ephesus, Philippi and Colosse he sent greetings
from the Christians in Rome. In his letter to the Colossians
there is quite a list of names but no mention of Peter. When
Paul wrote his final letter to Timothy he was near the end of his
life. He urged Timothy to come soon as he felt bereft with only
Luke as a companion. He added rather sadly, 'At my first
defence no one took my part; all deserted me, may it not be
charged against them' (2 Tim. 4:16). One can only comment
that if Peter was Bishop of Rome he was rather an absentee
from his diocese!

Is Peter the rock?

Returning to the main issue, the question to be discussed is
this: 'Is Peter the rock on which Jesus will build his church?'
Our reply to that question will be deeply influenced by the
principles of interpretation which we adopt. As far as Roman
Catholic students are concerned they have those principles of
interpretation clearly stated in the second article of the Creed
of Pius IV: 'Neither will I ever take and interpret them
otherwise than according to the unanimous consent of the
Fathers.' By 'the Fathers' of course is meant the great leaders
and teachers of the early centuries.

    This proves to be a solid barrier to interpreting this text as
Rome does, for if there is one thing that can be stated with

absolute assurance it is the simple fact that there was no unanimity in the interpretation of this text. Launoy, a seventeenth-century French Roman Catholic scholar, did a useful statistical survey of the varying views. Seventeen of the Fathers believed that the rock was Peter. Forty-four of them considered that it was Peter's faith, which had been expressed in his confession that Jesus was the Christ, the Son of the living God. Sixteen of them said that the rock was Christ and eight claimed that it referred to all the apostles. If the unanimity of the Fathers is the prerequisite to understanding the word 'rock' then we are in an impasse!

But there is more evidence to make this appeal to the Fathers a very dubious point! Augustine, one of the greatest theologians of those early centuries, actually changed his mind on the subject! In his early days he had thought the rock was Peter. But years later he acknowledged that he had also interpreted it as Peter's faith. But, to add insult to injury for the claimants for patristic unanimity, he added that it was up to each one to come to his own conclusion!

Yet we are told that this text underscores the sweeping claims of the papacy. We must surely ask in reply, if it was so patently obvious that Peter was the rock, then how was it that it did not appear clear to the Fathers, so that the present interpretation held by Rome was a minority view in the early church?

The reader may at this point feel like giving up in despair. If there is so much uncertainty, can we have any confidence in any interpretation? By way of response to that feeling of frustration I would point to a very basic way of endeavouring to interpret Scripture. If we face a difficult text then it can be a very profitable approach to find a text elsewhere on the same subject where there is no ambiguity. So we use the plain and obvious text as a key to unlock the more obscure verse. Which brings me to 1 Corinthians 3:11.

Paul states firmly and without any possibility of misunderstanding: 'No other foundation can any one lay than that which is laid, which is Jesus Christ.' The plain meaning is that Jesus Christ, and he alone, is the foundation of his church. This Christ is the one whom Paul and the others so faithfully preached. He is the Saviour who is revealed in all his glory by the apostolic testimony which itself is embodied in the New Testament.

With that starting-point we return to the seemingly diverse views of the Fathers. Perhaps they are not so much mutually contradictory as complementary to each other. Thus if Peter is viewed as the rock, it is Peter in his rôle at that very moment, bearing witness to Jesus as Messiah. But this faith was not Peter's alone, for it was the common response of all the apostles. Thus, whether we interpret the rock as Peter, or as Peter's faith, or as the content of his and the others' faith, we are converging on the point Paul made that the real foundation of the church is Jesus Christ.

Jesus has made a play on words. *Petros* is the Greek equivalent of Cephas in Aramaic, which was the disciples' vernacular. The rock is the feminine word *petra* so there is a distinction between the new rocklike discipleship to which Jesus had called him and the rock of his testimony, which was Christ. Lest anyone should misinterpret the verse to assert a special jurisdiction for Peter — which Rome in fact claims — Jesus rejects any notion of jurisdiction over the church apart from his own: 'I will build my church.' She is his church because the Father has given her to him (John 17:2,6,9, etc). She is also his church because he redeemed her by his blood shed at Calvary (John 10:11; Acts 20:28; Eph. 5:25). As Lord of his church he must have an unshared authority. Certainly Peter himself could not have seen Christ's words as conferring any jurisdiction, for in his first epistle he warned the elders with whom he associated himself as a fellow elder: 'Tend the flock of God that is your charge, not by constraint but willingly, not for shameful gain but eagerly, not as domineering

over those in your charge but being examples to the flock' (1 Peter
5:2-3). Peter had learnt well the lesson that universal jurisdiction belongs to Christ alone.

The keys of the kingdom

There still remains the final promise to Peter: 'I will give you
the keys of the kingdom of heaven, and whatever you bind on
earth shall be bound in heaven, and whatever you loose on
earth shall be loosed in heaven.' Rome claims that this indicates that an especial authority is given to Peter, not only 'to
govern the house of God', but 'to absolve sins, to pronounce
doctrinal judgements, and to make disciplinary decisions in
the church'.[2]

We shall examine this topic in more detail when we come
to look at the question of penance. For the moment, the issue is
papal authority, and a brief observation must suffice. Certainly
it is true that Peter was used to open the door to the Gentiles in
the meeting with Cornelius, but that was not his primary task,
as Paul pointed out (Gal. 2:7). Primarily Peter was 'entrusted
with the gospel to the circumcised', whereas Paul 'had been
entrusted with the gospel to the uncircumcised'. Peter, like
Paul and like the other eleven apostles, shared in this ministry.

An even stronger rebuttal of Rome's claims for Peter is
found in Matthew chapter 18, where the same authority is
given to the local church. When a Christian has been injured
in word or deed by a fellow believer he must try to set it right
with the offending brother. If he is refused he must take one or
two witnesses. If that fails he must go to the church, and if the
offender still refuses to hear the church he is to be barred from
communion. It is in this context of the life of a local congregation that the authority to bind or loose is committed.

But Jesus has a further compelling word. He applies this
concept of authority exercised on earth and ratified in heaven

to a small group — 'two or three' — gathered in prayer. Where
there is unity of spirit and an agreed concern, their praying on
earth is ratified in heaven. It needs to be stressed that this
parallel passage in Matthew 18:15-20 sets the words of Jesus
to Peter in chapter 16 in a far wider context.

If anyone argues that the authority of using the keys is not
in view here, one only needs to go back to Jesus' words in
Matthew 16:19. He clearly links the authority of the keys with
the authority to bind or loose. There is particular significance
in the link word 'and' in that Jesus said, 'I will give you the
keys of the kingdom of heaven, and whatever you bind on
earth shall be bound in heaven, and whatever you loose on
earth shall be loosed in heaven.' The two analogies of using
keys and binding and loosing are simply two ways of express-
ing the exercise of authority. The promise to the apostles is
extended to the local church and to every Spirit-prompted
gathering of those who have covenanted together in prayer.

Peter in danger (Luke 22:31-32)

Luke 22:31 uses the plural 'you' and clearly refers to all the
apostles, while verse 32 is in the singular and applies to Peter.
So Jesus first of all makes a general statement: 'Simon, Simon,
behold, Satan has demanded to have you [that is "all of you"]
that he might sift you like wheat, but I have prayed for you
[Peter] that your faith may not fail; and when you have turned
again, strengthen your brethren.'

A superficial reading of the two verses might suggest that
this is one more endorsement of the special rôle of Peter *vis-
à-vis* the other apostles. Certainly that is how the catechism
applies the statement to endorse a claimed authority for the
alleged successors of Peter. It quotes the *Lumen Gentium* of
Vatican II, which speaks of the claimed infallibility of the

pope. 'The Roman Pontiff, head of the college of bishops, enjoys this infallibility in virtue of his office, when, as supreme pastor and teacher of all the faithful — who confirms his brethren in the faith — he proclaims by a definitive act a doctrine pertaining to faith or morals.'[3] The key phrase here is in parenthesis: he 'confirms his brethren'.

Earlier in the catechism this notion of Peter's, and allegedly the pope's, strengthening ministry is highlighted by being linked to the Lord's resurrection appearance to Peter. This preceded the appearance to the other apostles. The conclusion is drawn by the catechism: 'Peter had been called to strengthen the faith of his brothers, and so sees the Risen One before them.'[4] This really is a dubious piece of exegesis. The writers might equally have stressed the point that Peter came second in the list, since the risen Lord appeared first to the women, and could therefore have drawn the conclusion that the latter had a special ministry! After all, Peter and John only went to the tomb because the women reported what they had seen (John 20:1-2).

There is, however, a much more straightforward way of approaching these verses in Luke 22. Instead of trying to squeeze them into a papally designed mould we should observe the basic principle of exegesis, and notice the immediate context in which Jesus was speaking. He was looking forward to the devastating impact that his death would have on the disciples. At the same time he recognized that such a time of trauma would provide an ideal situation for Satan to undermine their faith. This title of the tempter means 'the adversary'. The other often-used title, 'the devil', means 'the slanderer', or as he is described in the book of Revelation, 'the accuser' (Rev. 12:10). It was this pending attack which impelled Jesus to pray for them.

Simon Peter, however, came into prominence not because of his rôle as leader, but rather because he was going to be the biggest failure. The others would desert Jesus and flee for their lives, but Simon would deny him three times. The sinfulness of his denials would be compounded by the oaths he swore as he insisted that he didn't even know Jesus. Yet Simon had claimed so vigorously that he would stand firm. He even dared to compare himself favourably with the others: 'Even though they all fall away, I will not' (Mark 14:29). In spite of Jesus' specific prophecy of this threefold denial Peter's overweening confidence knew no bounds and with proud vehemence he insisted: 'If I must die with you, I will not deny you' (Mark 14:31). 'Lord, I am ready to go with you to prison and to death' (Luke 22:33).

When such pride is followed by such a fall the outcome can be acute spiritual depression. Peter's bitter tears were caused by the heartbroken realization that he had failed so deeply. Luke records the terrible moment when the cock crew, 'And the Lord turned and looked at Peter. And Peter remembered the word of the Lord, how he had said to him, "Before the cock crows today, you will deny me three times"' (Luke 22:60-61). Jesus had seen it all beforehand. He knew the accuser would accompany Peter into the darkness of the night, which must have matched the darkness in Peter's soul. To sin should always bring shame, but to sin in face of such pretensions as Peter had declared would bring overwhelming shame. How ready Satan would be to insinuate the thought that there was no forgiveness for this sin, no remedy for this failure! Judas succumbed to that temptation and killed himself. Peter by God's grace could seek and find pardon. How the Lord's words must have shone with new hope in his heart: 'I have prayed for you'!

So Peter was not singled out because of some imagined authority over the other disciples. It was rather because of the enormity of his fall and, what was even more serious, the possibility of being so slandered by Satan that he would plunge into despair. The weak attempt of the catechism to link the first glimpse of the empty tomb with his alleged special rôle is confronted with a much more satisfying explanation. Peter had failed more dismally than anyone else. He had been left to struggle with remorse and vain regrets. How gracious the Lord was to ensure that poor, humbled Peter would have a token of the Lord's forgiveness! So he was given an early testimony that the Lord had risen. But lest the old endemic pride should creep back, the women were the first witnesses, and it was they who pointed Peter to the empty tomb which would be the re-assurance his contrite and broken heart so deeply needed. The accuser was silenced for the conquering Saviour had risen. So Peter would strengthen his brethren, not by exercising dominion over them, but by displaying the sympathy of one who, having failed deeply, had been wonderfully forgiven.

It is the same response, and for a similar reason, which is recorded in Psalm 51. David had sinned most grievously. He had tried to cover up his sin and for months had battled with his conscience. Then the prophetic rebuke of Nathan laid him low. He pleaded with God for pardon and for cleansing that would make him 'whiter than snow' (Ps. 51:7). Like Peter he was a forgiven sinner, and like him also David could look forward with a deep confidence so different from the old presumptuous attitude: 'Then I will teach transgressors thy ways, and sinners will return to thee' (Ps. 51:13). So Peter emerged from the spiritual débâcle, not as the prince of the apostles, but simply as a pardoned transgressor who could humbly tell fellow sinners where forgiveness might be found!

Peter restored (John 21:15-17)

The risen Lord had appeared to the group of disciples by the lakeside. He had directed them to what proved to be a huge shoal of fish, and this was in contrast with the totally fruitless night they had spent. It was only then that it dawned on them that the figure on the beach was the risen Saviour. There was no vision. It was indeed a very physical encounter as the Lord had a breakfast of grilled fish for the hungry fishermen. It was after this breakfast that the Lord's interview with Peter took place. He did not address him by his new name of Peter but by the old designation, Simon. This must have recalled the first time by the lake when Simon Peter had responded to the call of Jesus to follow him. But there was a more recent memory which made Peter painfully aware of his own sad failure.

The initial question was painful enough. Peter had boasted that when the others failed he would stand firm. The penetrating question recalled that empty boast: 'Simon, son of John, do you love me more than these?' All Peter could say in reply was: 'Yes Lord; you know that I love you.' The reply of Jesus was a fresh mandate: 'Feed my lambs.' It was at one and the same time an assurance of forgiveness, but also a reminder that gentleness, rather than his former arrogance, was needed to tend the lambs of the flock.

But the question was repeated: 'Simon, son of John, do you love me?' This time the comparison with others was omitted so he could put behind him the shame of his earlier boastfulness. His reply was simply a repeated affirmation: 'Yes, Lord; you know that I love you.' His assurance of restoration was deepened as the Lord repeated his pastoral mandate: 'Tend my sheep.'

The Lord, however, was not yet finished. So the question was repeated for the third time: 'Simon, son of John, do you love me?' That thrice-repeated question was so painful. It recalled so vividly Peter's threefold denial which had made such nonsense of his earlier professions of loyalty. It is no wonder that 'Peter was grieved because he said to him the third time, "Do you love me?"' All he could do was to fling himself on the tender mercy of his Saviour: 'Lord, you know everything; you know that I love you.' It was as if Peter was acknowledging the shame and grief of the past and yet clinging to the Lord's forgiving grace and affirming with a new humility his deep love. His joy must have been overflowing as the Lord repeated the commission: 'Feed my sheep.'

Sadly the Vatican Catechism tries to manipulate this loving interview with Peter to draw from it the extraordinary implication that Jesus was affirming Peter's leadership over the other apostles and the unique commission to feed the flock of God. So it claims: 'The Lord constituted him shepherd of the whole flock.'⁵ 'Jesus the Good Shepherd confirmed this mandate after his resurrection.'⁶ How much more straightforward is the view of a long line of commentators, from early writers like Gregory Nazianzen or Cyril of Alexandria down to the present time! They have seen the threefold questioning as recalling the denial. As far as the feeding of the flock is concerned, this is exactly the same mandate as Paul gave to the elders in the church at Ephesus, who were commissioned, exactly as Peter was — after all he called himself a 'fellow elder' (1 Peter 5:1) — to 'care for', or 'feed', 'the church of God' (Acts 20:28).

The testimony of the rest of the New Testament

The interpretation of these three passages from Matthew, Luke and John fits in with what the rest of the New Testament has to say about Peter. Thus when the conference in Jerusalem was convened to hear the complaint from the church in Antioch about the false teaching emanating from Jerusalem, it was James, not Peter, who was in the chair. This was not James the apostle, for he had been killed by order of Herod (Acts 12:2). Peter made his contribution, and so also did Paul and

Barnabas, but it was the overseer of the local church who presided.

The situation described in Galatians 2 is rather similar. Peter had been led into a virtual endorsement of the false teaching which was rejected at the conference in Jerusalem; hence his withdrawal from fellowship with Gentile believers. Clearly Paul did not see Peter as the infallible head of the church. Indeed, he went so far as to rebuke Peter publicly: 'I opposed him to his face, because he stood condemned' (Gal. 2:11). Can you imagine a cardinal openly rebuking the pope and then mentioning the matter in a letter which would be circulated among the churches? Paul's rebuke is an emphatic rejection of any notion that the New Testament churches recognized Peter's primacy.

5.
Radicals in Rome

The word 'Inquisition' brings back memories of Catholic Spain and the barbarous torture and cruel deaths of great numbers of victims. It may surprise many that the 'Holy Office', as it was called, has a continuing successor today in the 'Congregation for the Doctrine of Faith'.[1] Of course it no longer uses the rack and the thumbscrew, nor does it have the freedom it once enjoyed to hand over its victims to a Catholic state for execution. It is still active, however, and has a powerful rôle in maintaining the traditional faith of Rome.

The congregation met in December 1979 to examine two leading liberal, or radical, theologians, Edward Schillebeeckx and Hans Küng. There was a firm insistence that it was not a trial but a *colloquium* — the English word is 'conversation'. However, to an observer it looked remarkably like a trial! The examiners acted like judges, but the defendant, or 'conversationalist', did not know in advance who they would be. Schillebeeckx was to discover that one of his examiners, a Jesuit, had already attacked him on Vatican Radio, virtually calling him a heretic.

That was not all. Not only was one examiner apparently allowed to pre-judge the issue, but none of the three examiners was acting in the rôle of spokesman for the accused. Even worse, from the point of view of the two men, the rôle of the spokesman for the defence was confined to an earlier phase of the investigation and there was no requirement for him to be present at the formal enquiry. After all, this was not a trial — though to most outsiders it looked very much like one, and an unjust one at that.

The outcome was predictable. Both men were found guilty. Küng had his authority to teach as a Roman Catholic theologian revoked. Schillebeeckx was allowed to continue but obviously he was under suspicion. The reason why his trial, or 'conversation', had less drastic results than that of Hans Küng was probably due to the angry intervention of Cardinal Willebrands, president of the Dutch bishops' conference. His protest against the trial was not matched by any similar action on the part of the German bishops and Küng was condemned.

Küng may also have been treated more harshly because he had dared to question fundamental Roman beliefs. Some eight years earlier, in 1970, his book *Infallible?* was published. It was a devastating attack on the dogma of papal infallibility which he claimed was brought in at the First Vatican Council to spite the modernists. He not only queried the very citadel of papal authority, but challenged the authorities to rethink their whole position. The next year saw another attack in his book *Why Priests?* The whole priestly and sacramental system of Rome was under frontal assault. But Küng was to discover that you might reject biblical truths and get away with it, but you were asking for trouble when you probed the bitterly defended dogmas at the heart of the papal and hierarchical system.

If I were simply writing about Küng and Schillebeeckx I would query their unbiblical position in other areas. Küng's denial of the virgin birth and the bodily resurrection is typical of his radical rethinking of Scripture. Schillebeeckx also seems to be closer to those who reject the Gospels' record of an objective, factual resurrection and an empty tomb, in favour of a subjective explanation — in other words, that the disciples experienced the resurrection power of Jesus in their lives. For such men the empty tomb may or may not be a historical fact. My reason for introducing them here is in order to show the methods used by the Vatican and, more importantly, to look at Küng's claims that there is a counter-revolution in full swing at the Vatican.

The Second Vatican Council certainly gave strong evidence that a new surge of challenges to accepted traditions was under way. When the council was convened it was obviously not to the taste of the ecclesiastics in Rome who, like civil service establishments elsewhere, prefer the even tenor of established procedures rather than the threat of challenge and rebellious questioning.

John XXIII had summoned the conference with the aim of opening the windows of the Vatican and letting a breath of fresh air circulate. The air came, however, not as a gentle breeze, but as a much more turbulent storm! The cut and dried formulae prepared by the Vatican establishment were firmly rejected and a new debate was introduced. There were bishops present, particularly from northern Europe, who had brought with them their *periti,* their theological experts. The latter enjoyed a liberty such as had not existed for generations. The results may be seen in the documents of Vatican II, which are in some ways a compromise between the traditionalists and the modernizers. But such compromises tend to be of a temporary nature, as one side endeavours to regain old ground while the other tries hard to break new.

John's successor Paul VI was to spend a lot of time and energy trying to roll back the victories of the progressives. His encyclical *Mysterium Fidei* was a reaffirmation of the old views of the Eucharist and his *Marialis Cultus* endeavoured to give a vigorous endorsement to the cult of Mary. The summons back to the old ways was seen in his *Credo of the people of God*, with its reminder and reinforcement of traditional dogmas.

John Paul II followed suit, spending much of his energy trying to bring Rome back to the old way. The radicals, however, have moved more and more into influential teaching positions in the seminaries and this has ensured the development of a radical appraisal of the dogmatic system.

The question arises as to the source of this new counter-revolutionary spirit, as Küng described it. Certainly John XXIII had given the radicals an opening. After the ultra-conservative rule of Pius XII, John drew a vital distinction which proved to be a rallying call for the progressives. He spoke the key words at the opening of the council: 'The substance of the ancient doctrine of the deposit of faith is one thing, and the way in which it is presented is another.'[2] In other words, the actual dogma is one thing and its expression is another. So it would be possible for a liberal to claim to be loyal to Rome while undermining papal authority and Catholic dogmas by reinterpreting them.

The rise of modernism

While the council provided the forum and John furnished the opportunity, the radical movement did not suddenly spring into being. The ferment had been going on for a long time — since the beginning of the twentieth century, if not during the later stages of the nineteenth. Indeed, Vatican I in 1870 had heard rebellious voices raised at the imposition of papal infallibility. One of the council members, Bishop Strossmayer, made a devastating attack on the proposed dogma, while others withdrew early from the council meetings to avoid the embarrassment of having to vote openly against the pope. The surge of modernism — the word was first coined in Catholic circles — came a few years later and for an account of this we need to go to France.

France and the Vatican have not always had an untroubled relationship! The early fourteenth century saw the climax of a long-running quarrel between the Vatican and Philip IV of France, who asserted his rights to tax the clergy, and so challenged Boniface VIII's claims to be sovereign over kings and rulers. Boniface was driven from the papal throne by the French. Later in that century France provided a home in Avignon for the popes from 1309 to 1377, and when the great papal schism broke out it was France who welcomed the alternative popes. This phase lasted from 1377 until 1408, when the papacy returned to Rome.

The seventeenth and early eighteenth centuries saw the rise of the Jansenist movement, with its strong affirmation of the sovereignty of God. Its headquarters at Port Royal were finally closed down by Clement XI in 1713. An even greater blow to papal power came with the French Revolution of 1789, which left behind many abiding consequences, including the secularist and anti-clerical thinking of much subsequent French history.

It is not surprising therefore to see the term 'Gallicanism' applied to radical thinking which is viewed by traditionalists as subversive of papal claims. Significantly, the alternative and traditionalist pattern, with its submissive attitude to papal claims, was designated 'ultramontane', across the mountains — that is, Italian!

The movement inherited a tradition of French independence — France had not accepted the decrees of the Council of Trent. The four Gallican articles drafted by Bishop Bossuet aimed to avoid a clash with the Vatican. They were accepted by a special synod of clergy in 1682 and asserted the sovereignty of the king in all things temporal, the subordination of the pope to a general council and also to the legal requirements of the French king. A fourth article gave the pope spiritual authority but still qualified this authority by making it subject to correction in its exercise within the realm of France.

Gallicanism had its heyday in the seventeenth century but its mood lived on in the rejection by the French revolutionary leaders of clerical authority, a rejection only partly modified by the concordat between the Vatican and Napoleon.

Among the distinguished opponents at the First Vatican Council to the declaration of papal infallibility, Dupanloup, Bishop of Orleans, was one of those who were ready to face papal disapproval for their resistance. The resistance, of course, was unsuccessful, but it was one more link in the history of French refusal of Vatican traditionalism.

One great cause for regret is that the greatest Frenchman of them all reaped a rich harvest across the world, yet was excluded by persecution from reaping in his own homeland. Jean (John) Calvin, from Noyon in Picardy, was the outstanding theologian of the Protestant Reformation in the sixteenth century. His achievements went far beyond Gallicanism, with its attempts to moderate Rome and to trim the papacy to a more acceptable level. Calvin was prepared to take the challenge to Rome to its utmost points, as he rigorously carried through the implications of accepting the Bible as the supreme authority to which he appealed.

Returning to the long saga of French protests, we come to the beginning of the twentieth century and the rise of a movement which Calvin would certainly have totally rejected. The radical reassessment of the gospel was rooted in rationalism. Its attacks on the supernatural had already had a widespread influence on the theological schools of Germany, where the so-called 'higher criticism' was undermining the very foundations of the Christian gospel.

The subsequent movement in Rome was given the title 'modernism'. Its leader was a Frenchman, Albert Loisy. He had not only rejected specifically Catholic dogmas, but had adopted the rationalism of the higher critics. The inerrancy of Scripture was rejected and the great gospel truths were robbed of their supernatural content. He was, of course, only part of a much wider movement which was to have such devastating consequences in the churches of the Reformation.

The pope was still in a position to exercise a vigorous discipline which contrasted with the flabby compromise of many Protestant leaders. It was no wonder that Ronald Knox, son of an evangelical Bishop of Manchester, quit the Church of England because of its tolerance of modernism, and joined Rome because of its firm handling of modernist teaching.

Loisy renounced his priestly function in 1906 and two years later repudiated the Christian faith. Pius X acted. Loisy was excommunicated. The encyclical *Pascendi* condemned modernist teaching and was followed by the imposition of the anti-modernist oath in 1910. Sadly, Pius could only try to counter modernism by such suggestions as more frequent attendance at mass, greater devotion to Mary and early first communion for children. Where the situation cried out for a positive affirmation of biblical truth, he could only offer traditions. He may have congratulated himself that he had sounded the death-knell of modernism. In fact the movement continued underground. It was like the drainage in limestone country where a stream disappears from view but percolates through the strata to re-emerge later, perhaps a considerable distance away.

There was an ongoing attempt in the years ahead to counter any theologians who strayed out of line. Pius XII made it very clear that his judgement was the final criterion by which theologians could assess their teaching. The encyclical *Humani Generis*, issued in 1950, firmly asserted that when the pope has come to a conclusion on any doctrinal issue the matter is no longer open to debate by theologians. This encyclical prepared the way for the issue of the dogma defining the assumption of Mary. In Pius' view, if the pope spoke on the subject the issue was closed.

Pius seems to have been convinced that submission to papal authority was widespread and that the spectre of modernism had disappeared. So he concluded the encyclical with great confidence: 'We are fully satisfied that the majority of Catholic teachers, employed in universities or seminaries, or religious houses of study, are untouched by these errors; errors which have spread abroad, openly or in secret guise, as the result of an itch for modernity, or indiscreet zeal. But we know that up-to-date speculation of this kind may easily attract the unwary; better to deal promptly with the first symptoms than to seek remedies later on for a disease now firmly established.'[3] How wrong he was, as events were yet to show!

We return to our starting-point, which was the indictment of two prominent theologians, Schillebeeckx and Küng. They were, of course, only two among many others who might be described as progressives or radicals. Teilhard de Chardin, Karl Rahner and many others could be cited. We need to try to discover what these progressive writers have in common. Of course there are divergences. The Latin Americans, who struggle with the poverty, exploitation and injustice of their countries, have a different agenda from their European contemporaries. Their theology of liberation, with its revolutionary undertones, is a reaction to a situation which is remote from that confronting the seminarians of the USA or Europe. The latter are facing the materialism and greed of the Western world, coupled with the paganizing of largely secularist societies and the emergence of all kinds of esoteric cults.

Back to the Bible

In face of all this confusion there has been a welcome recognition by Rome of the need to get back to the Bible. So Bible-reading is encouraged, whereas not so many years ago it was forbidden. Bible-study groups seem to be increasingly evident. This is all positive in that the greatest need today, as indeed it has been in every age, is to hear what the Word of the Lord is saying to this generation. Amos, the rugged prophet, speaks to our generation from his standpoint eight centuries before Christ's coming. He describes our own situation in vivid terms:

'Behold, the days are coming,' says the Lord God,
  'when I will send a famine on the land;
not a famine of bread, nor a thirst for water,
  but of hearing the words of the Lord'

(Amos 8:11).

It was in face of that dearth that Amos brought the people, not his own opinions, but the prophetic word which God had entrusted to him.

Does this all mean, with Bible-reading being encouraged and progressive Catholic churches making appeal to Scripture, that all is well? Far from it! The word of Scripture may be read, but it is often distorted by church traditions, or by contemporary philosophy. We have already considered, in chapter 3, the distortion of the message that arises if one accepts the conclusion of Vatican II that Scripture is only part of the revelation which also requires ecclesiastical tradition and the papal teaching office.

It is, however, not only tradition and the presumption of papal authority that must be challenged, but the liberal appeal to Scripture which is then modified by humanist considerations. The result is that man becomes the measure of truth rather than being the humble learner who reads the Bible to hear what God is saying. Earlier in this chapter I suggested that the appeal of the new thinkers to the Bible is deeply qualified by their own presuppositions. This approach is like looking at a landscape through heavily tinted spectacles.

For example, in liberation theology there is an underlying assumption that the main summons of Jesus is to challenge the exploitation of the poor and to pronounce judgement on the structures of society imposed by the rich. Thus for the proponents of this view, the key Bible book is Exodus, with its history of the liberation of Israel and their journey to the promised land. So Jesus becomes the revolutionary figure, a latter-day Joshua.

It is certainly true that Jesus was scathing in his denunciation of rich exploiters. Likewise Paul gives justice an important place in the Christian's reflections on life (Phil. 4:8). James echoes the same message in his devastating rebuke to the rich who exploit the poor and to the hypocrisy of the church which gives a warmer welcome to those who are socially acceptable (James 2:1-4; 5:1-6). Yet beyond all this emphasis on justice there is a far greater stress — it is on the sinful state of both rich and poor, the lost condition of all without exception. Jesus is pre-eminently the Saviour from sin and the agent for reconciling rich sinners and poor sinners to God. Once that basic reconciliation is accomplished, those now renewed by the Spirit of God become brothers and sisters. It is not so much the structures of society that need change but the human heart.

I have referred to liberation theology primarily in terms of an illustration of the false approach which imposes a pattern on Scripture. One sees a similar imposition by people like Küng and Schillebeeckx and, of course, many others. Their underlying assumption seems to be that we come to Scripture, not as humble learners needing the enlightenment of the Holy Spirit, but as those already steeped in contemporary philosophy, the basic tenets of which we accept as our starting-point. This leads to the kind of approach which a humanist critic might apply to the examination of any ancient document from the Latin or Greek classics.

If we begin with the exaltation of human reason, inevitably we shall fail to hear what God is saying. One recalls Jesus' rebuke to the Sadducees, with their rationalism, and to the Pharisees, with their religious traditions: 'Truly, I say to you, the tax collectors and the harlots go into the kingdom of God before you' (Matt. 21:31).

Behind so much of what used to be termed modernism and is now referred to as radical thinking, there is a tendency to deny the supernatural. So the miraculous events are queried and the books of the Bible become the attempts of particular men to express their religious experiences. One can understand therefore why Schillebeeckx wrote as he did. There is, in his writing, clear evidence of the influence of the Protestant radicals, with their hesitancy to affirm a doctrine as true. So he would claim that a particular doctrine is true only in so far as it acts as a signpost to a greater truth which is unknowable.

But if the greater truth cannot be known how can we be sure that the signpost is pointing in the right direction? If it is pointing into a fog we are left with total uncertainty. If, on the other hand, a bright light is illuminating the goal then we are in a position to assess the correctness or otherwise of the sign! By contrast with this approach, which begins with men trying to probe the unknown, the Scriptures are presented to us as coming from God: 'No prophecy ever came by the impulse of man, but men moved by the Holy Spirit spoke from God' (2 Peter 1:21).

Küng is even more forthright than Schillebeeckx. We have already noted his rejection of the virgin birth and the bodily resurrection of Jesus. We might add his rejection of the authenticity of parts of Scripture which do not fit easily with his underlying position. For example, he does not consider Matthew 16:18-19 as authentic. He does not believe Jesus exercised the baptizing ministry as described by John (John 4:1). Nor does he accept Luke's record that Paul and Barnabas

ordained elders (Acts 14:23) — on the grounds that the
account does not fit in with his assumption that Paul's view of
the church is not institutional but charismatic.

The agreement of these radical Catholic writers with many
Protestant theologians is seen in other areas, notably in their
misinterpretation of the incarnation and in the issue of
universalism. The Bible teaches that the Son of God took our
nature and became one of us so that he might endure the
penalty of our sins and accomplish on our behalf a perfect
righteousness. 'For our sake he made him to be sin who knew
no sin, so that in him we might become the righteousness of
God' (2 Cor. 5:21). Their misinterpretation leads to the false
inference that Jesus thereby sanctified the whole of life, thus
abolishing the distinction between secular and sacred, between world and church. The result is an 'incarnational theology' which fails to do justice to the biblical view of the
devastating consequences of sin, both in humans and in
creation, with a corresponding failure to appreciate the need
for atonement.

Universalism, the teaching that all will ultimately reach
heaven, has a long history. The main reason why it has been
rejected is that it runs contrary to the continuing thrust of the
Bible, which warns of hell, opens the way to salvation through
Christ alone and presents, especially in the teaching of Jesus,
a solemn picture of a final Day of Judgement and for many an
eternal exclusion from the presence of God.

We might well wonder how the radicals could evade plain
biblical teaching. They do so by invoking the truth that God is
love and ignoring the equally firmly stated truth that he is holy.
He is not only a gracious heavenly Father, but also 'a consum-
ing fire' (Heb. 12:29).

Again we might well ask about the clear scriptural teaching
on the absolute necessity of faith. Their reply would doubtless
follow the line of distinguishing between implicit and explicit

faith. The latter is the faith exercised by the sinner who sees Jesus Christ as the only Saviour and trusts in him. Implicit faith, we are assured, is in the religious aspirations of those who do not accept the Christian message. Indeed Kevin McNamara goes so far as to say, 'It is possible for the atheist in good faith to be numbered among those who love God and despise self.'[4]

Hans Küng would agree. He wrote, 'The resurrection of the crucified Christ which the Church believes and preaches is the proclamation of the resurrection of all men and of the renewing of the world.'[5] A powerful rebuttal of this can be found in both the Old Testament and the New. Daniel writes, 'Many of those who sleep in the dust of the earth shall awake, some to everlasting life, and some to shame and everlasting contempt' (Dan. 12:2). Jesus echoes that sombre message again and again, distinguishing between 'eternal punishment' and 'eternal life' (Matt. 25:46). The New Testament ends, not only with the glimpse of 'a new heaven and a new earth', but also of 'the lake that burns with fire and sulphur, which is the second death' (Rev. 21:1,8).

The gospel has always been an affront to human pride. It insists that there is only one way of salvation. It points to Christ, not as one more figure in the religious market-place, but as the one and only and all-sufficient Saviour. Jesus himself made plain in completely unambiguous words his claim to uniqueness: 'I am the way, and the truth, and the life; no one comes to the Father, but by me' (John 14:6). Peter made the same claim in face of the hostility of the Sadducees: 'There is salvation in no one else, for there is no other name under heaven given among men by which we must be saved' (Acts 4:12). Paul presented the same exclusive claims for Jesus Christ to the philosophers in Athens: 'God ... now ... commands all men everywhere to repent, because he has fixed a day on which he will judge the world in righteousness by a man

whom he has appointed, and of this he has given assurance to
all men by raising him from the dead' (Acts 17:30-31).

That is why the church of Christ has always been, from its
very beginning, a missionary body aiming to point men and
women from every tribe and nation to the one way of salvation.
During the centuries of Christian history each fresh stirring of
spiritual life in the churches has prompted a new surge of
missionary endeavour. However, the new radicalism in Rome
sees that mission in a new light. In a symposium to celebrate
the fiftieth anniversary of the Maynooth Mission to China a
different note was struck — one which emerges, not from the
New Testament, but from the attempt to integrate the Bible
into modern thought. So Enda McDonagh claimed — and one
can hear the echo of universalism: 'Jesus proclaimed the
intention of the Father of making all men sons.'[6] Such an aim
clearly alters the agenda for missions. So McDonagh claims
that non-Christian religion has much to teach us, so that both
missionary and non-Christian leaders are working together:
'We do not come to distribute our riches but to work with them
towards a fuller grasp for both of us of the only riches that
matter, the riches of Christ. We are as willing to listen as to
preach.'[7] This is a far cry from the missionary passion of the
apostle Paul, whose heart longed for the salvation of those he
declared to be 'separated from Christ ... having no hope and
without God in the world' (Eph. 2:12).

This kind of teaching is widespread and appears in unex-
pected ways. John Paul II accepts all the vast claims for the
pope to be the focal point of the saving work of the gospel: 'It
is absolutely necessary for the salvation of all men that they
submit to the Roman Pontiff' (Bull *Unam Sanctum* of
Boniface VIII). Yet still the pope has had well-publicized
discussions with the Dalai Lama and appeared at a multi-youth
gathering in Assisi together with non-Christian leaders, to
pray for peace. Mother Theresa is constantly in the limelight.

Not so well known is the fact that her hospice in Calcutta is on Hindu temple property, or that she is in the forefront of the multi-faith movement. She introduced to the congregation of St James Piccadilly the so-called 'prayer of peace', which is based on Hindu holy books. It is to be addressed to whatever deity one may choose! Perhaps Küng and Schillebeeckx and their many friends and supporters have penetrated even further than either they or the Vatican realized!

6.
The church and the papacy

The catechism begins well! 'The word "church" means a convocation or an assembly.' It is also correct in seeing that the church of the New Testament is in direct succession from the Old Testament assembly of the people of God — the translators of the Septuagint, the Greek version of the Hebrew Scriptures, had used the Greek word *ecclesia* to translate 'assembly'. That word would bring to mind an assembly in a Greek city convened for a civic purpose. So the church in Corinth or Ephesus is an assembly of the people of God convened by the Holy Spirit. Each local assembly is the visible appearance of the church of all the ages of history and a foreshadowing of the great assembly in heaven.

However, the departure from the New Testament soon eclipses the encouraging beginning. For example, the claim is made that the church is structured hierarchically. The Greek word *hiereus* means 'a priest' and it is most significant that a New Testament pastor, also called 'elder' or 'overseer', is never designated 'priest'. The task of the ministry is to feed the flock of God with the Word of God but never to offer a sacrifice on their behalf.

The continuing incarnation?

Even more serious error emerges as the totally unbiblical claim is made that 'Christ and his church together make up the "whole Christ" [*Christus totus*] ... we have become Christ... Head and members form as it were one and the same mystical person.'[1]

This view of the church is not some doctrinal innovation but reflects speculation which had gone on for a considerable time. Back in the nineteenth century Mohler, the German theologian could write, 'Here is his Church, his institution in which he continues to live, in which the Word uttered by him continues to echo for ever. Thus the visible Church, seen from this point of view, is he who is continually seen among men in human form, who is ever renewing himself, the Son of God who is eternally being rejuvenated, his permanent Incarnation.'[2]

It was at this time that Rome's views of the church and the papacy were preparing the way for the defining of papal infallibility at Vatican I. The intertwining of church and papacy was given an enormous boost which was to culminate with the publication in 1943 of Pius XII's encyclical *Mystici Corporis*, which identified the Roman Catholic Church with the mystical body of Christ: 'And so to describe this true Church of Christ — which is the Holy, Catholic, Apostolic, Roman Church — there is no name more noble, none more excellent, none more divine, than the mystical Body of Jesus Christ.'[3] Pius went so far as to claim: 'He [i.e. Christ] so upholds the Church and so, after a certain manner lives in the Church that she may be said to be another Christ.'[4]

Paul VI echoed this in a speech at Vatican II where he claimed that the church is 'Christ's continuation both earthly and heavenly'. He went on to say, 'Christ is our founder and head. He is invisible yet real. We receive everything from Him and constitute with Him the whole Christ.'[5] His claims were echoed by the Second Vatican Council: 'We must not think of the Church as two substances, but a single complex reality, the compound of a human and a divine element. By a significant analogy she is likened to the mystery of the Word incarnate: the nature taken by the divine Word serves as the living organ of salvation in a union with Him which is indissoluble.'[6]

Because this all seems akin to Paul's references to the church as the body of Christ, the unwary might think that the council and the catechism are being eminently biblical. That is far from the truth. In the New Testament there is a very emphatic distinction between Christ, the head seated in glory (Heb. 10:12-13), and the limbs of his body here on earth. The limbs are the individual members of his church, truly indwelt by the Holy Spirit but still deeply aware of their own sinfulness. While the light of the Spirit has shone into their hearts yet there are still shadows in their understanding, for at best, 'I know in part' (1 Cor. 13:12). To fail to distinguish between the head and the limb is to fail to recognize that Christ is without sin and he alone has final authority in his church.

Outside this church there is no salvation — this claim made by Boniface VIII in 1302 is asserted afresh. The conclusion is drawn that 'All salvation comes from Christ the Head through the Church which is his body.'[7] Allowance is made for those who through no fault of their own do not know Christ and his church — that is, the church as defined in the catechism. It is the old Roman qualification of 'invincible ignorance'. Someone, like the present author, who is fully aware of Rome's claims and rejects them would be in a really tenuous position! It seems to be akin to the saying: 'Where ignorance is bliss 'tis folly to be wise.'

Mother and teacher

The identification of the church as the continuing incarnation of Christ has many serious implications. So the claim is made: 'From the Church he [the Christian] receives the Word of God... From the church he receives the grace of the sacraments.'[8] It is not surprising that the church is presented as 'Mother and Teacher'. So it is claimed that it is through the sacraments of the church that we receive spiritual life and by that same means this life is sustained. The word of Scripture that we receive comes, so it is claimed, from the church, which is the source of truth.

The New Testament speaks another message. It is not that by union with the church we are saved. Peter's preaching recorded in Acts 2 made such an impact on the hearers that they cried out, 'Brethren, what shall we do?' The response is plain: 'Repent, and be baptized every one of you.' Significantly, repentance must precede baptism! Those who were saved as they responded to the word were added to the church: 'The Lord added to their number day by day those who were being saved' (Acts 2:47).

The same emphasis is seen earlier, in John's Gospel. Those who experience the miracle of spiritual new birth do not owe their new life to the church, but directly to the Holy Spirit: 'To all who received him, who believed in his name, he gave power to become children of God; who were born, not of blood nor of the will of the flesh nor of the will of man, but of God' (John 1:12-13). The church's task is to bear witness to Christ and to call sinners to repentance and faith. But there must be no intermediary between the sinner and the Saviour. 'There is one God, and there is one mediator between God and men, the man Christ Jesus' (1 Tim. 2:5).

Turning to the notion that the church is teacher, we find the idea that the church gave us the Scriptures: 'From the Church he [the Christian] receives the Word of God.'[9] If this simply meant that we normally hear the Word either via the preaching of that Word, or through the personal witness of someone who has already embraced that Word, we might accept it. But Rome moves beyond that by teaching that the Scriptures are not uniquely the revelation from God, but are supplemented by the tradition of the church and are to be understood as they are interpreted by the magisterium — that is, the teaching authority within the church. We are back to the basic idea that the church is a structure governed by the pope and by the bishops in fellowship with him.

All this runs contrary to the whole pattern of both Old and New Testaments. In the Old Testament the prophets are the mouthpiece, not of the people of God but of God himself. When they speak it is as those set apart to address the assembly with divine authority. Hence we hear the often-repeated introduction: 'Thus says the Lord.' Amos, in a great passage, faced the priests of his day who queried his authority. He acknowledged that he did not have the ecclesiastical status demanded by his critics, who lightly granted that status to the false prophets. Yet he had something more important than that: 'I am no prophet, nor a prophet's son; but I am a herdsman, and a dresser of sycamore trees, and the Lord took me from following the flock, and the Lord said to me, "Go, prophesy to my people Israel"' (Amos 7:14-15).

The New Testament pattern is just the same. The apostle Peter rejected the notion of a human initiative: 'No prophecy ever came by the impulse of man, but men moved by the Holy Spirit spoke from God' (2 Peter 1:21). Paul wrote to the Galatians and rooted his authority, not in the church but in the direct mandate from God: 'Paul an apostle — not from men nor through man, but through Jesus Christ and God the Father, who raised him from the dead' (Gal. 1:1). When John wrote the letters to the seven churches in Asia Minor, it was as the mouthpiece of God bringing the churches under scrutiny or encouragement or rebuke. The constant refrain sums up the truth that the church is under the authority of the Word: 'He who has an ear, let him hear what the Spirit says to the churches.' One recalls a vivid comment of Martin Luther that the church is the daughter born of the Word, not the Word's mother.

Infallible?

This reference to the teaching authority within the church brings into focus another emphasis in the catechism's doctrine of the church, namely the infallibility of the pope and the diffused infallibility of the bishops, who claim to act and teach as the successors of the apostles in fellowship with the pope, already designated as successor of Peter. We have already seen the complete absence in the New Testament of any mention of successors to Peter. There is the same absence of any reference to apostolic succession.

This is not, however, simply an argument from silence, for there is positive biblical warrant for saying that the apostles did not have any successors. Indeed, we may go further and say that by definition they *could not* have any successors, for fundamental to the call to be an apostle was the fact that they were to be eyewitnesses of the risen Lord. The catechism admits this: 'In the office of the apostles there is one aspect that cannot be transmitted: to be the chosen witnesses of the Lord's resurrection.'[10] Yet having acknowledged the uniqueness of the apostolic eyewitnesses, it proceeds to contradict this in the very same paragraph with the statement quoted from Vatican II in *Lumen Gentium*: 'Therefore the apostles took care to appoint successors.' The justification for this is an appeal to two scriptures which in fact have not the remotest link with any notion of apostolic succession. One of these is Matthew 28:19: 'Go therefore and make disciples of all the nations.' It is a distortion to make 'disciples' mean 'bishops'. Acts 11:26 reminds us that 'In Antioch the disciples were for the first time called Christians.'

The other scripture quoted to justify the theory of a succession of bishops is Acts 20:28, Paul's mandate to the elders in Ephesus: 'Take heed to yourselves and to all the flock, in which the Holy Spirit has made you overseers.' Far from supporting apostolic succession, this passage demolished the whole notion of a diocesan bishop! The word translated 'overseers', or 'guardians', is *episcopoi*, which may be translated 'overseers' or 'bishops' — hence the term 'episcopate'. The snag for the Vatican's appeal to this verse is that the passage makes clear that elder and bishop are interchangeable terms. The word 'elder' speaks of a man's standing in the congregation and the term 'bishop' refers to the nature of his ministry. It is not surprising then that Paul wrote, 'To all the saints ... who are at Philippi, with the bishops and deacons' (Phil. 1:1). He was not ignoring the elders for the simple reason that elders and bishops were one and the same!

There is a significant note in the Catholic Revised Standard Version which makes the point very clearly. In a note on 1 Timothy 3:1 it refers to the office of a bishop and comments: 'At this time an office probably not distinct from that of priest.' Apart from the fact that the correct translation is elder (presbyter), it is good to see the admission that the office of a diocesan bishop is a later development for which the authentication is based on an appeal to tradition, but certainly not to the New Testament. Incidentally in this whole discussion the catechism is quoting from the documents of Vatican II. It is in the *Dogmatic Constitution on the Church* that apostolic succession is asserted (Chapter III, para. 20). To quote the council, however, does not make 'apostolic succession' valid. It simply shows how far the council diverged from the Bible!

Writing before the withdrawal of his authority to speak as a Catholic teacher, Hans Küng made a trenchant criticism of these grandiose claims for the church: 'Christ is the head and remains the head, which controls the body. The concept of head always carries overtones of the ruler. The body can only exist in total dependence on him. It is of vital importance for the Church that it allows Christ to be its head, otherwise it cannot be his body.' Earlier in the same book he pointed out that 'A Church which falsely identified itself with the Holy Spirit turns itself into a revelation.'[11]

This claim for the church — and of course it is the Roman Catholic Church which is in view — is no peripheral issue. In fact it is the most basic tenet of Rome for from it springs so much of her other teaching. After all, if Christ is present in terms of a continuing incarnation it must be Christ in all his Messianic power. The very title 'Christ', the Greek rendering of the Hebrew 'Messiah', means the 'Anointed One'. So it takes us back to the Old Testament and to the offices for which men were anointed, that is to say, set apart for a special ministry.

The prophet

The prophets were anointed by the Holy Spirit. Isaiah made this explicit claim: 'The Spirit of the Lord God is upon me, because the Lord has anointed me' (Isa. 61:1). In that claim he was echoing the rest of the prophets of the Old Testament. It is therefore most significant that Jesus took those words of Isaiah and made them his own. He was the culmination and the fulfilment of the ministry of the prophets of the Old Testament. He did not abrogate their claims or qualify their message. Rather he presented himself as the one to whom they had pointed and the one who would bring to a triumphant fulfilment all that they had said. Hence his decisive claim, 'I am ... the truth' (John 14:6), and hence also the recognition by the New Testament writers that he was God's final word to men and women!

The letter to the Hebrews opens with the glad acknowledgement that 'God spoke of old to our fathers by the prophets.' This is immediately followed by the assertion that now 'He has spoken to us by a Son.' This decisive and final revelation is God's last word. What will be required now is reflection on the revelation and a response in terms of discipleship. For both those responses we are promised the Holy Spirit's enlightenment. He will bring understanding to the simplest believer but it will not be a case of adding further revelations but of disclosing the full glory of the message so conclusively given by Christ.

Once concede the notion of a continuing incarnation and you are faced with the totally erroneous notion that the prophetic ministry of Christ goes on. On that basis all the dogmas which have emanated from Rome are given a spurious validity as the claim is made again and again that when the church speaks, Christ speaks. One might well observe that the supposed revelations and infallible disclosures are qualified. They are only claimed to be infallible when the conditions are right — when the pope speaks *ex cathedra* (from the papal throne) and when he is claiming to be defining a dogma as being binding on the universal church. This is a strangely qualified claim to infallibility which is in sharp contrast with the New Testament, where the whole Word is binding without qualification.

The priest

Returning to the anointed ministries of the Old Testament we find a key rôle being played by the priests, with their head the high priest. Basically the priestly task was to act as mediator between the people and God. The priest confessed their sins and voiced their praise. But above all he offered the sacrifices on their behalf. The whole pattern of Levitical sacrifice stressed the need for sin to be punished and reconciliation to be achieved. So the sacrificial victim from the flock or herd was the sin-bearer. The ritual reached its annual climax on the Day of Atonement, when the high priest entered the most holy place in the temple and sprinkled the atoning blood on the mercy-seat.

This symbolism, or if you like, this picture language, pointed forward to the New Testament, when the Son of God would be anointed by the Holy Spirit as both priest and victim. John the Baptist recognized him as 'the Lamb of God, who takes away the sin of the world' (John 1:29). The letter to the Hebrews takes up the theme of priesthood and works out in detail the rôle of the High Priest from heaven who offered the final sacrifice and, having presented himself in the heavenly sanctuary with his own atoning blood, then sat down at the right hand of God (Heb. 7-10).

Rome, however, distorts this revelation of the great and final High Priest offering the one decisive sacrifice. Instead, the theory of a continuing incarnation points to a priest who continues to offer himself. We shall come back to this in greater detail when we come to consider the eucharist. At this point I would simply emphasize that Rome fails to see how decisive an event was the ascension of Jesus. After the resurrection the risen Christ appeared to his disciples, not in vision but in reality. These appearances and this continuing presence came to a dramatic end when from the Mount of Olives he ascended into heaven. The New Testament is clear — the next appearance and functioning of Christ on earth will be the Second Coming, to which the angel pointed as he reassured the perplexed disciples (Acts 1:11). Hence Christ is now in glory. He does not need to offer any other sacrifice since his perfect offering has been accepted. Meanwhile before he returns, he is not the absent Christ for he is present, just as his Father is present, through the indwelling presence and power of the Holy Spirit who 'proceeds from the Father and the Son'.[12]

We shall return to this issue later but meanwhile we must look at the third ministry in the Old Testament for which men were anointed.

The king

The king was in fact designated 'the Lord's anointed'. It was this divinely conferred rôle that made David recoil from acting when he had King Saul at his mercy. He rejected Abishai's readiness to kill the king and replied in words he had used before: 'Do not destroy him; for who can put forth his hand against the Lord's anointed, and be guiltless?' (1 Sam. 26:9). After all, according to Old Testament teaching, the king was not simply head of state and commander-in-chief of the army. He was pre-eminently the Lord's representative. His office as the Lord's anointed was intended to represent to the nation the sovereign rule of the Lord over his people.

Sadly, many of the kings failed in their task. Their kingship mirrored to the people, not divine justice and benevolence, but human pride, lust and corruption. Even the best of them, such as David or Hezekiah, had serious failures in their records. It is no wonder that increasingly the hope developed that the King of kings would come and display with perfect righteousness the sovereign rule of God Almighty. One can appreciate therefore the explosive significance of the preaching of John the Baptist: 'Repent, for the kingdom of heaven is at hand' (Matt. 3:2). It was the trumpet-blast announcing the advent of the Messianic king. When Jesus repeated precisely the same message (Matt. 4:17) it was the public declaration that the Messiah had come and the rule of heaven was embodied in his person and his work.

With the victory of the resurrection and the climactic event of the ascension, the dominant theme of the New Testament is the proclamation of the Lord of glory who sets up his kingly rule in the hearts of his people and will finally display it in his Second Coming when 'Every knee [shall] bow, in heaven and on earth and under the earth, and every tongue confess that Jesus Christ is Lord, to the glory of God the Father' (Phil. 2:10-11).

Once again we find the truth distorted as the theory of a continuing incarnation sets the kingly rôle of the Messiah within the present world-order. It is not simply the perfectly biblical teaching that Christ rules within his church and his authority is gladly accepted by Christians. Rather it is misused to give Rome a spurious justification for her prominent political rôle. So the Vatican is organized like any other earthly state. It has its secretary of state and all the departments of government. It has its foreign service with its diplomats accredited to the various nations. The old three-tiered tiara of the pope was a visible declaration of his claim to a universal episcopate, a universal jurisdiction in the church and an authority over kings and presidents. So, like other realms, the Vatican state makes treaties — the concordats with Hitler, Mussolini and Franco were among the most unsavoury treaties of the twentieth century.

Lest anyone should imagine that these concordats were simply for show, we should note the outcome of the disastrous policy of the Vatican Bank. Its head, Archbishop Marcinkus, was protected from the Italian police who wanted to interrogate him. Another Vatican financial adviser, Sindona, got a long prison sentence in the USA. However, Marcinkus escaped scot-free as the concordat with Mussolini led to the Italian supreme court cancelling the arrest warrants against him and two other senior bankers.[13]

Governments rely a great deal on their intelligence service, whether the American CIA or the British MI5. The Vatican has its own information-gathering facilities and its own methods of bringing pressure to bear on national leaders. One of these effective agencies is the shadowy Opus Dei. The title of the organization means 'the work of God', which it identifies with the interests of the papacy. It has opponents within Rome but John Paul II proved to be a wholehearted supporter of it. A society of lay people under the tight control of priests was

obviously an attractive body from the standpoint of a pope
who knew how to operate the levers of power. In 1982 he put
the order beyond the control of any diocesan bishop. The
technical procedure was to give it the status of a prelature,
which virtually treated the order as a separate diocese. The
previous year saw the first step being taken to canonize the
order's founder Escriva. Clearly the pope saw Opus Dei as a
significant agency.

Vatican political intrigue has been going on for centuries.
Twentieth-century means of communicating around the world
have simply added one more tool to the armoury. There have
always been influential figures in business, the media and
political life who have been willing collaborators. The failure
of Marxism and the break-up of the Soviet empire in Eastern
Europe have given further opportunities for intrigue.

The façade of religious activity has often concealed very
irreligious strategies. At the end of the Second World War
Cardinal Roncalli already had friendly links with von Papen,
the notorious Nazi. Roncalli was active in covering up past
ecclesiastical co-operation by French bishops with the Nazis.
So he helped to get them off the hook! They had supported the
pro-Nazi regime in Vichy after the fall of France. Paul
Touvier, the fellow-worker of Klaus Barbie, the notorious
'butcher of Lyons', was kept from justice for years in various
religious houses. The genial Roncalli who charmed the world
as Pope John XXIII was a skilful operator and not too choosy
about his agents. He even appointed von Papen as Papal
Chamberlain.

Another country which suffered greatly was Serbia. The
Croatian leader Pavelic was appointed by the Nazis and was
supported by Cardinal Stepinac. The outcome was the mass-
acre of huge numbers of Serbs who, unhappily for them,
belonged not to the Roman communion but to the Greek
Orthodox. The Serbs clearly have never forgotten! When the

war ended and war criminals were facing trial Pavelic escaped. The infamous 'rat route' devised by the Vatican for such men was via religious houses in Italy to Roman Catholic countries in South America.

The whole sordid business has gone on for so long that many books have been written on the subject. Yet amazingly, as a result of ecumenical euphoria and skilful propaganda, the papacy is seen by so many as a wonderfully benevolent institution, taking a strong moral stance in a degenerate world. How far that image is from the truth! The sufferings of a great multitude cry out for exposure of the whole sorry story — the slaughtered Jews of Austria, where the cardinal welcomed the Nazis; the victims of Himmler, himself trained by the Jesuits; the deportees from Lyons despatched by Touvier. The only reply to those cries is the solemn hour of God's coming judgement.

Against all this we hear the voice of Jesus: 'My kingship is not of this world; if my kingship were of this world, my servants would fight, that I might not be handed over to the Jews; but my kingship is not from the world' (John 18:36). Earlier, when he was betrayed, he checked the impulsive Peter who with his sword was going to try to deliver his Master. The Lord's firm words, 'Put your sword into its sheath' (John 18:11), find an echo in Paul's reminder to the Ephesians that our defence is not earthly power, nor do we use physical or political means to achieve gospel ends. Our key weapon is 'the sword of the Spirit, which is the word of God' (Eph. 6:17).

7.
Catholic Pentecostalism

The title of this chapter is already rather dated. Yet in the early days of the movement it was a regular designation. René Laurentin from France and Kevin and Dorothy Ranaghan from the USA used the titles *Catholic Pentecostalism* and *Catholic Pentecostals* respectively. Edward O'Connor, another American priest, had a similar though rather more lengthy title: *The Pentecostal Movement in the Catholic Church.* I have retained the title though I am fully aware that 'the Charismatic Renewal' or, more simply, 'the Renewal' would be more contemporary. My reason for doing so is to emphasize the significance of the change in designation.

Cardinal Suenens of Belgium, author of *Ecumenism and Charismatic Renewal*, must have seen the disadvantage, from his point of view, of the earlier titles. Clearly they indicated the very close links between the emergence of the Roman Catholic movement in the late sixties and the older Pentecostalism with its roots in the nineteenth-century holiness churches and the awakening on New Year's Day 1901 in the Bible School in Topeka, Kansas. From Topeka the movement spread across the world and led to the emergence of such denominations as Elim, Assemblies of God and the Apostolic Church.

Suenens was emphatic that the movement in which he was involved — and, indeed, recognized as a leader — must be distinctively Roman Catholic and must therefore stand apart from what he would term the fundamentalism of classical Pentecostalism. He stressed the basic position: 'We believe that the Catholic Church is the Church in which the one Church of Jesus Christ subsists in its entirety.' By contrast, other churches are 'imperfectly integrated with what we regard as the trunk of the tree planted by the Lord'. [1]

Suenens attempted, as did others, to align the charismatic movement with traditional Roman dogmatic teaching. Baptismal regeneration was firmly reasserted — the pentecostal experience was the conscious entry into the new life which 'the sacraments of Christian initiation had already deposited in us germinally, but [which] now rises to full consciousness'.[2] He put this in plainer terms when he rebuked those in Catholic circles who claimed, 'I became a Christian on such and such a day,' with an allusion to being baptized in the Spirit. He was emphatic: 'A person who was sacramentally baptized as an infant became a Christian from that day.'[3]

We find the same emphasis when he deals with submission to the pope and loyalty to Rome. Thus he stresses the doctrine of the real presence: 'Those who receive Holy Communion at a Catholic Mass not only receive the Body and Blood of Jesus Christ, but also publicly express their unity with the pastors of the Catholic Church, primarily the bishops and the Pope.'[4] Needless to say, there is an equally strong affirmation of the centrality of the cult of Mary. Indeed the latter is presented not as a stumbling-block but as a 'welcoming haven of reconciliation'.[5]

It must not be assumed that uneasiness with the Catholic/ pentecostal link began with Cardinal Suenens. Nor must we conclude that he was the first to attempt to integrate the movement more firmly with loyalty to Rome. Right from the outset the leaders of the movement not only gave indications of their Catholic background but in fact declared as their stated

aim the cultivation of a distinctively Roman Catholic piety.
Thus Edward O'Connor, writing in the early 1970s, found the
term 'pentecostal' unsatisfactory even though he used it in the
title of his book. His continued employment of the term was
because 'It is by now so firmly attached that there is little
chance of shaking it off.'[6] He says he is more disposed to use
the title 'charismatic movement'. He must have been relieved
when that title prevailed and it was much easier to highlight the
essential Roman Catholicism of the movement.

The movement began in university circles in the USA. The
first leaders were laymen and there was obviously a danger of
a church within a church. Clearly they needed to reassure the
bishops that they were authentically Catholic. Hence it is not
surprising that there was such a firm insistence on basic
Catholic doctrines and on thoroughgoing submission to epis-
copal authority.

Much that happened in the early days elicited a warm
response from evangelicals in the Protestant churches. They
saw a strong commitment to Bible study together with a
seeming readiness to implement the biblical truths in the life
of the charismatic fellowship. There was also a spontaneity in
prayer which was far removed from the rigidity of the Roman
liturgy. Here were men and women claiming that they were
trusting in Christ, and in Christ alone, for salvation. Surely it
was a time, not for carping criticism, but for glad acceptance
of what had the marks of a true work of grace.

A word which seems so fitted to the situation is the message
of Paul to the Thessalonians: 'Do not quench the Spirit, do not
despise prophesying' (1 Thess. 5:19-20). That should check
any tendency to adopt a dismissive attitude. It is also a
reminder that it is a very serious matter to reject out of hand
what claims to be a work of the Holy Spirit. One recalls the
warning of Gamaliel to his fellow members of the council who
had been interrogating the apostles, and indeed displaying an
enraged rejection of their testimony. Gamaliel's sobering

comment pointed to their danger: 'You might even be found opposing God!' (Acts 5:39).

This, however, does not mean an unqualified acceptance of every claim to spiritual experience that is enthusiastically made. Paul, after all, qualified his warning to the Thessalonians not to quench the Spirit with the necessary additional charge: 'But test everything' (1 Thess. 5:21). That attitude is reflected in the New Testament epistles. Of course there was encouragement, and indeed thanksgiving to God, when there was evidence of growth in holiness. At the same time there was a sober appraisal and a readiness to rebuke when false teaching was corrupting the life of the church, or when dubious additions to worship or deviations from righteous living were tarnishing the witness of the church.

It may seem at first sight a difficult, or indeed impossible task, since we are unable to see into the heart of another Christian. Paul's firm challenge meets us here: 'Why do you pass judgement on your brother? Or you, why do you despise your brother? For we shall all stand before the judgement seat of God' (Rom. 14:10), However, while I dare not presume to give God's verdict on the inner state of another professed believer, the gospel of Christ yet commits me to assess what is in the public domain, namely the teaching which this Christian presents. After all, there was evidence of spiritual life in Galatia, yet false teaching had so corrupted the church that Paul had to pose his grieving question: 'You were running well; who hindered you from obeying the truth?' (Gal. 5:7). Indeed he even had to criticize both Peter and Barnabas for their failure to act consistently with the truth.

The Spirit of truth

What is clearly needed is a standard by which to assess teaching, preaching, or any claimed prophetic word. The best

starting-point for discovering this standard is found in Jesus'
designation of the Holy Spirit. He spoke again and again of the
Spirit and used the title 'the Spirit of truth' (John 14:17; 15:26;
16:13). John, in his first epistle, used the same phrase which he
had used in the Gospel — hence it seems more correct to read
1 John 4:6 with the capital 'S', 'the Spirit of truth', thus
echoing the earlier usage. This designation underlines the
consistency of the Spirit. He does not have to retract what he
has revealed. He does not contradict himself by revealing new
teaching which runs contrary to what has already been disclosed.

Where then do we find the perfect revelation made by the
Spirit of truth? It has been the steady conviction of Christians
down the ages that the Scriptures of the Old and New Testaments are precisely that revelation. That certainly was the
conviction of Jesus himself — witness his constant appeal to
Scripture to corroborate his teaching; witness also his insistence that 'Scripture cannot be broken' (John 10:35), and his
rebuke to the Sadducees: 'You are wrong, because you know
neither the scriptures nor the power of God' (Matt. 22:29). The
plain implication of his words was that if they had known the
Scriptures they would not have gone astray. He was echoed by
the apostles, with their high view of Scripture as being 'God-
breathed' and given through men who were 'moved by the
Holy Spirit'. (I have already touched on this in chapter 3.)

This emphasis on the Holy Spirit as the Spirit of truth is
especially important because the devil is 'the spirit of error'
(1 John 4:6). Jesus branded Satan as 'a liar and the father of
lies' (John 8:44), since he often 'disguises himself as an angel
of light' (2 Cor. 11:14). Because he is the arch-deceiver we
must be on our guard when the Holy Spirit is powerfully at
work, for that so often is the occasion for satanic counter-
attack which may come, not in some spectacular fashion, but
in the subtle infiltration via minds that have been deceived.

It is therefore essential that we test every claim by means of the standard which the Holy Spirit sets for us. Since he cannot contradict himself the obvious conclusion is that every true prompting by the Spirit must by definition echo what he has revealed in the Scripture. The corollary is that any utterance or teaching within the church which is contrary to the Spirit-revealed truth in the Scripture cannot be accepted as true.

Allied to this constant emphasis on the primacy of truth, there is also a firm insistence on the primacy of the mind, which is the means by which we receive the truth. Isaiah brought God's summons in these terms: 'Come now, let us reason together, says the Lord' (Isa. 1:18). God calls us to use our minds to consider the gospel. Paul echoed this call when he wrote to the church in Rome, 'So faith comes from what is heard, and what is heard comes by the preaching of Christ' (Rom. 10:17).

Of course, the apostle recognized the condition of the unregenerate: 'The god of this world has blinded the minds of the unbelievers, to keep them from seeing the light of the gospel of the glory of Christ' (2 Cor. 4:4); but he rejoiced at the same time that God's regenerating power had restored their ability to think clearly about God's truth: 'For it is the God who said, "Let light shine out of darkness," who has shone in our hearts to give the light of the knowledge of the glory of God in the face of Christ' (2 Cor. 4:6).

The key rôle of the mind in conversion is continued as the Christian matures in holy living. So the apostle presents the Christian life as one of spiritual transformation which is achieved 'by the renewal of your mind' (Rom. 12:2). He wrote in similar vein to the Colossians, 'Set your minds on things that are above' (Col. 3:2). The church in Philippi received the same message: 'Finally, brethren, whatever is true, whatever is honourable, whatever is just, whatever is pure, whatever is lovely, whatever is gracious, if there is any excellence, if there is anything worthy of praise, think about these things' (Phil. 4:8).

I have laid special emphasis on the primacy of the mind in responding to the truth. This is not in any sense to belittle the emotions and the fervour of spiritual experience, but rather to reflect the order of experience as it is presented in the Scripture. There the truth received by the renewed mind arouses the conscience and stirs the emotions to deeply-felt experiences — whether sorrow over sin, glad delight in God's forgiveness, or sheer joy in God himself. At the same time this order of spiritual growth acts as a check on purely emotional responses. Of course, when the Spirit moves within us there will be a great stirring of our feelings. But because he is the Spirit of truth he will keep reminding us that we must assess our experiences not simply by their intensity, but by whether they are consistent with the truth which the Spirit has brought through our minds.

It is precisely in this area that charismatic experience must be tested. Failure to do this can lead deeply astray, as may be seen in the case of the Dominican Simon Tugwell. He saw no biblical warrant for the teaching of 'baptism in the Spirit', but he still claimed that the experiences of so many pointed to much wider implications. His commitment to Rome gave him a vision of the rôle which Roman Catholicism, and especially the charismatic movement, could play. He claimed that the Second Vatican Council pointed towards a sharing with 'all our separated brethren' in order to achieve what he called 'wholeness'.

Then came his extraordinary claim: 'Marxism, Zen, Transcendental Meditation, Pentecostalism, all sorts of things may help us on our way as we seek to enter into our inheritance of wholeness.'[7] Here is a repudiation of Jesus' unique claims: 'I am the way, and the truth, and the life; no one comes to the Father, but by me' (John 14:6). Here also is a rejection of the apostle Peter's exclusive claim for Jesus Christ: 'There is salvation in no one else, for there is no other name under heaven given among men by which we must be saved' (Acts 4:12). Tugwell revealed how he reached such erroneous conclusions when he admitted: 'We read the Bible inevitably in the light of our experience.'

The commentators in the early days of the charismatic renewal in Rome — or as they would then have described it, Catholic Pentecostalism — were particularly insistent on its consistency with Roman Catholic teaching. This was seen especially in three areas: the rôle of Mary, the doctrine of transubstantiation and the supreme authority of the papal office. As these three issues are dealt with in other chapters in this book I will, in this chapter, simply note the claims made in these areas which, I believe, contradict the testimony of the Spirit of truth. That, after all, was the approach which drew special commendation by Luke as he referred to the Bereans who did not accept unthinkingly the preaching even of the apostle Paul, but 'received the word with all eagerness, examining the scriptures daily to see if these things were so' (Acts 17:11).

Devotion to Mary

That kind of constructively critical attitude was sadly lacking in the early days of Catholic Pentecostalism. We are presented with anecdotes describing experiences, but the evidence does not come under the scrutiny of Scripture. This is especially so in the realm of devotion to Mary. One such experience was recorded in describing the fellowship at Notre Dame University. Someone spoke in what was claimed to be a tongue — this was their first experience of the phenomenon. Another student declared that while the utterance was taking place, 'The words, "Holy Mary, Mother of God, pray for us sinners" kept running through my head.' Then he added with firm assurance: 'I feel moved to tell you all that what Mary promised at Fatima is really going to take place.'[8]

The response within the meeting developed further. One woman who acknowledged that she had formerly been repelled by devotion to Mary, now declared that 'Since receiving the baptism in the Spirit she had become more open to it.' But more was to follow. A priest claimed that in 'the tongue' he had distinctly heard the Greek words *'Chaire Maria'* (Hail Mary). It was only the next day — so the author claims — that anyone realized that since it was the festival of the Annunciation (the visit of the angel to Mary to announce the birth of Jesus) the charismatic session of the previous evening had been 'a vigil' of preparation for the festival!

Leaving aside the issue of Mary for consideration in a later chapter, one must draw attention to a basic fallacy in the whole account. The apostle Paul could not have been more explicit when he stated that 'One who speaks in a tongue speaks not to men but to God' (1 Cor. 14:2). He emphasized the point that, by contrast, 'He who prophesies speaks to men' (1 Cor. 14:3). Yet O'Connor totally ignores this truth since there is an uncritical acceptance that 'the tongue' was addressed to Mary, who clearly is not God!

There is a further fallacy. If a tongue is specifically directed to God, as Paul insists it must be, then any interpretation must yield an appropriate utterance focused on God, whether of penitence, praise or adoration. Such utterance would necessarily be fitting in words directed not to men but to God. But the error is compounded, for the alleged interpretation presents a very human message of a promised fulfilment of an alleged appearance of Mary at Fatima. The interpretation was directed to the members of the fellowship group. In fact it is interpreted as if the original utterance was a prophecy. O'Connor tries to meet this problem by introducing the notion of another function called 'a message in tongues'. There is no biblical warrant at all for this claim. He explains that it might be called 'prophecy in tongues'. If we accept Paul's teaching we can only dismiss this phrase as a contradiction in terms!

René Laurentin had the same emphasis on devotion to Mary. There is the same failure to take Scripture as the ultimate criterion. It is true that he appeals to Ephesians 1:3, where Christians in general are described as blessed, or highly favoured. It is the same word as the one which the angel used in announcing the birth of the Saviour. So Mary was 'highly favoured', and so also are all Christians. To take the faulty Latin of the Vulgate translation with its *'plena gratias'* (full of grace) is to miss the point completely, in that grace is God's gift to all his people. Laurentin's comment, when he expounds Ephesians 1:3, that Mary is the 'object *par excellence* of God's favour'[9] is a lame one. There are simply no grounds for saying that while Ephesians 1:3 speaks of God's favour to us all, it was more specifically directed to Mary.

Laurentin seemed to see his mission as being to stir the English-speaking charismatics to the same pattern of fervent devotion as he saw in France. It is not surprising therefore to discover that he presented Mary as the 'Model of the Charismatic'.[10] He deduces this partly from the fact that she was specified by name as being in the upper room on the Day of Pentecost. Since Luke records at length in his Gospel the nativity stories and since Luke was the author of Acts, he reads Mary's charismatic, and indeed prophetic, rôle into Luke's account of the Day of Pentecost.

He does not, however, explain Luke's total silence on the subject of Mary for the remainder of the Acts. We might also note that Luke described Anna as a 'prophetess' (Luke 2:36), but did not thus designate Mary. Then again there is the whole detailed examination of the issue of charismatic gifts in 1 Corinthians 12-14. The man who wrote those chapters was a fellow worker with Luke. How often Paul and his very close friend must have discussed the great event of Pentecost and the subsequent supernatural happenings! It is incomprehensible that there should be an acknowledged 'model of the charismatic' and that Paul should either have been ignorant of this, or should have failed so completely to point to that model for our imitation. It would be like a teacher of English literature knowing of the great sixteenth-century model and yet totally failing to quote Shakespeare!

Laurentin had the honesty to admit that there is no biblical evidence for the dogmas of the immaculate conception and the assumption. There is likewise no evidence for claiming that Mary was a prophetess. Laurentin produces the very weak argument that because the song of Zechariah is specifically designated as prophecy, therefore the song of Mary must also be a prophetic utterance, even though Luke does not describe it in that way. However, the absence of evidence in Scripture does not silence Laurentin's claims, which are shored up, not by Scripture but by tradition — hence his assertion: 'Besides a weighty tradition originating in the Greek and Latin Fathers attributed to Mary the title "prophetess".'[11]

Eucharistic devotion

The focal point of Roman Catholic worship is the eucharist, and the underlying dogma which turns the eucharistic feast of remembrance into the 'sacrifice of the mass' is the dogma of transubstantiation. The notion is that the substance of the bread and wine is miraculously transformed at the consecrating words and actions of the priest, to become the substance of the body and blood, soul and divinity of our Saviour. The application of this teaching is varied, whether it is a requiem mass for the repose of the departed, a nuptial mass for what is claimed to be the sacrament of marriage, or a mass offered with 'a special intention' — that is, in order to meet some specific need.

Closely related to this is the issue of devotion to the reserved sacrament. In face of the many liturgical changes in eucharistic worship the veneration of the sacrament was not only emphasized but explained by Paul VI in his *Mysterium Fidei*, issued on 3 September 1965, just before the fourth session of the Second Vatican Council. He could not have been more explicit as he claimed: 'Not only in her teaching has the Catholic Church maintained belief in the presence of Christ's body and blood in the eucharist, but in her life as well. For there has never been a time when she has failed to venerate this great sacrament with the cult of worship which is due to God alone.'[12]

He then added further emphasis to his claim that worship due to God is implied in veneration of the sacrament by pointing to other practices: 'This cult of worship which ought to be bestowed on the sacrament of the eucharist has been offered by the church outside as well as within the rites of the Mass, she still does so, by taking the greatest care in preserving consecrated Hosts, presenting them to the people for their solemn veneration, carrying them in processions to the joy of the people in their crowds.'

Detailed discussion of these issues must await later chapters. What is in view here is the reaction to such teaching by Catholic charismatic leaders. Far from their raising queries about any elements of either the dogmas or the devotional practices there seems to have been an enthusiastic acceptance of them. Far from moderating the excesses of unbiblical practice the charismatics seem to have endorsed them whole-heartedly. Simon Tugwell goes so far as to quote favourably from the renowned thirteenth-century Dominican Thomas Aquinas that 'If there had been a consecrated host reserved at the time of Christ's death, we should have to say that he died also in the reserved host'[13] (the word 'host' is from the Latin *hostia* — that is, victim).

Typical testimonies are given by Kevin and Dorothy Ranaghan: 'Attendance at daily mass has grown to be my way of life.' 'This experience of communal prayer in the spirit of the Psalmist has in no way jeopardized concern for, or participation in, the institutional life, the sacramental realities or the traditional devotions of the Church.' 'The Mass has become much more meaningful and personal to me since having received this infusion of new life.'[14]

Edward O'Connor has similar testimonies. A nun referred to her experience of praying in tongues, and said that 'She could do so only when alone in the presence of the Blessed Sacrament.' A student at Duquesne University, Pittsburgh, described how 'He felt powerfully drawn towards the tabernacle by a force that seemed almost physical. The presence of Christ on the altar seemed to dominate the entire chapel, and draw everything towards itself.' He went on to recount how 'He spent an hour or more in wondering adoration before the Blessed Sacrament.'[15] All this forces one to ask how the Spirit of truth could possibly be invoked to authenticate practices and doctrine which are so remote from the Scriptures which the Spirit moved the New Testament authors to reveal.

Loyalty to the institutional church

It is not surprising that in general the movement has received such a warm welcome from the hierarchy in view of its obvious commitment to the structures of the church. An early and slightly cautious welcome was given by the American bishops. The committee on doctrine of the National Conference of Catholic Bishops presented their report in 1967. They were obviously anxious to distinguish it from Protestant Pentecostalism. At the same time they voiced their approval of the way that members of charismatic prayer groups seemed 'to grow in their attachment to certain established devotional patterns such as devotion to the real presence and the rosary'. The conclusion they drew was that the movement should be encouraged but under the supervision of the bishops and of designated 'prudent priests to be associated with this movement'.

Cardinal Suenens followed this pattern. We saw earlier how he strongly emphasized the depth of the divergence from Protestant Pentecostals. He recognized the reality of ecumenical activity but insisted that Catholic charismatics should, among other requirements, remember 'their relation to Mary and the saints as part of their whole Catholic life', and also 'the mentioning in prayer of the Pope, the bishops and other specific Catholic intentions'. Further reminders are required lest in a charismatic conference pentecostal members who were not Roman Catholics should assume unity too lightly. They must be gently but firmly reminded that they cannot share in the eucharist because 'Those who receive Holy Communion at a Catholic Mass not only receive the Body and Blood of Jesus Christ, but also publicly express their unity with the pastors of the Catholic Church, primarily the bishops and the Pope.'[16]

Edward O'Connor spoke in similar terms as he pointed to what he saw as the value of tradition as it had developed under the guidance of the popes. It is not surprising therefore that he viewed the possibility of any charismatic quitting Rome as a false step. Such people, he wrote, 'are following a delusion'.[17] He applied the same strictures to those who fulfil the requirements 'minimally'. This is a sobering rejoinder to evangelicals who claim that their charismatic Catholic friends do not really agree with some Roman Catholic dogmas and practices. Such 'minimalism' is not permitted!

In case anyone should object that many of these quotations come from books published in the early days of the movement it might be useful to end this section by quoting from a widely acclaimed book by a very prominent Catholic charismatic leader. It was published in 1994! He refers to 'the gold' which endures when 'the dross' is consumed. We ask him what is the gold preserved by Rome. His answer is very clear: 'For the Roman Catholic Church the structures of universal communion in baptism and eucharist, in the threefold ministry of bishop, priest and deacon, and the primatial ministry of the pope as successor to Peter are part of the gold, gifts of the Spirit of God essential to the constitution of the Church in this world.'[18]

The path to Christian unity involves what Peter Hocken calls reintegration. Pope John had the same notion in mind when in his encyclical *Ad Petri Cathedram* he invited Protestants to return to their ancestral home in Rome. Catholic charismatics have seen the movement as heaven's answer to the pope's prayer for a new Pentecost. We can only reiterate the importance of seeing Pentecost as a visitation by the Spirit of truth. The movement and the churches need to return to submission to the truth. The old slogan *'Sola Scriptura'* is sorely needed.

8.
Mary

When, in 1974, Pope Paul VI issued his 'Apostolic Exhortation' on the cult of Mary *(Marialis Cultus)* he was not breaking new ground. He declared his desire 'to enhance devotion to the Blessed Virgin Mary', and in his attempt to achieve that goal he was following an increasingly well-trodden path ever since Pius IX declared the dogma of the immaculate conception of Mary in 1854, and one down which even greater numbers would follow during the next couple of decades. As we saw in earlier chapters, not only traditionalists but radicals and charismatics have indicated with varying degrees of enthusiasm their commitment to what even a Roman Catholic charismatic called 'Marian piety'. The cult of Mary has flourished. I use the term 'cult', not in some pejorative sense but strictly echoing the title of Paul VI's exhortation.

John Paul II and the cult of Mary

The cult was given even greater impetus by John Paul II who has declared again and again his utter devotion to Mary. His prayer *'totus tuus'* — 'completely yours' — was not directed to God the Father, nor to Christ the Lord, but to the woman who has taken the place of the true Mary of Nazareth, and who seems to dominate so greatly his devotional life.

In his book written as a series of answers to a journalist's questions he explained that to pray, 'I am completely yours, O Mary,' meant an 'attitude of total abandonment to Mary'.[1] This certainly is a far cry from Paul's attitude of total abandonment to Christ: 'For to me to live is Christ, and to die is gain' (Phil. 1:21). Paul wrote to the Christians in Rome urging total commitment to the Lord: 'I appeal to you therefore, brethren, by the mercies of God to present your bodies as a living sacrifice, holy and acceptable to God' (Rom. 12:1), but the papal message from that same city urges total commitment to Mary.

John Paul II describes in his book how his passionate devotion to Mary developed. As a child he often stopped before the image of 'Our Lady of Perpetual Help' in the parish church which was 'tied to the tradition of the Carmelite scapular'.[2] He was referring to the medieval legend that in 1251 Mary appeared to an Englishman, Simon Stock, on Mount Carmel telling him that deliverance from hell and from purgatory was sure for those who wore the scapular, a piece of woollen cloth worn under the clothes and upon the shoulders.

He recalls with approval the dying words of Cardinal August Hlond as he looked forward to the deliverance of Poland from Communist domination: 'The victory, if it comes, will come through Mary.' John Paul applies this to the future of the worldwide church and echoes and amplifies the cardinal's words: 'If victory comes it will be brought by Mary. Christ will conquer through her, because he wants the church's victories now and in the future to be linked to her.'[3]

There is not a scrap of biblical evidence for these fanciful claims. What a contrast it is to listen to Jesus himself saying, 'I will build my church' (Matt. 16:18), or to give heed to the apostle Paul's vision of final victory: 'He [that is, Christ] must reign until he has put all his enemies under his feet' (1 Cor. 15:25). John Paul points to his native Poland and claims: 'The Polish nation has sought for centuries, and continues to seek support and strength for spiritual rebirth from its Lady and Queen.' Could there be a more decisive reply to all this than Paul's words of triumphant praise: 'But thanks be to God, who gives us the victory through our Lord Jesus Christ'? (1 Cor. 15:57). God has exalted his Son above all others: 'He has put all things under his feet and has made him head over all things for the church' (Eph. 1:22). Like the apostle John on the island of Patmos we see Christ's unique splendour and sing, 'To him be glory and dominion for ever and ever. Amen' (Rev. 1:6).

Even when he is dealing with other issues John Paul constantly harks back to the issue of Mary. In his 'Holy Thursday' address of 1979 he urged bishops and priests to look to Mary: 'You must look to her with exceptional hope and love.' He adds that she will teach them about Christ and puts the question: 'Who will better communicate to you the truth about him [i.e. Christ] than his mother?'[4] How totally false this is, since the one who communicates all knowledge of Christ to us is the Holy Spirit! Jesus himself made that so plain when he spoke of the 'Spirit of truth' who would guide them into the truth: 'He will glorify me, for he will take what is mine and declare it to you' (John 16:14).

Later that year John Paul issued his exhortation *Catechesi Tradendae* dealing with the handing on to others of the teaching of Christ. He called for a dynamism in this teaching ministry. Where is this dynamism to be found? His answer is in a prayer to Mary: 'May the Virgin of Pentecost obtain this for us through her intercession.' He does recognize that the presence of the Holy Spirit is needed, but the way to experience the Spirit's power is to have recourse to 'the prayer of Mary'.[5] Again he parts company with Jesus, who linked the coming of the Holy Spirit with his own prayers and with the willingness of the Father to give the Spirit: 'I will pray the Father, and he will give you another Counsellor, to be with you for ever, even the Spirit of truth' (John 14:16-17). 'If you then, who are evil, know how to give good gifts to your children, how much more will the Heavenly Father give the Holy Spirit to those who ask him!' (Luke 11:13).

In his letter to the bishops on the 1600th anniversary of the First Council of Constantinople, John Paul is back to his constant theme: 'When the Church was born by the power of the Holy Spirit in the upper room in Jerusalem, she began to look to Mary as the example for her own spiritual motherhood.'[6]

If that was the case it is quite extraordinary that after the passing reference to her in Acts 1:14 Mary totally disappears from view in the remainder of the New Testament. There is not the slightest indication in any epistle that Mary was to be the model for godly living. But then, for the apostolic writers, the only model was Jesus Christ himself. Our summons to run the race set before us is accompanied by a reminder of the stimulus — we are to keep on 'looking to Jesus the pioneer and perfecter of our faith' (Heb. 12:1-2).

John Paul has demonstrated his 'Marian piety', not only in his preaching and writing, but in his obvious zeal in going on pilgrimage. When he spoke at Knock at the centenary celebrations of the alleged appearance of Mary in 1879, he recalled how important in his own life had been his pilgrimages to the shrines in various countries. He has been to Guadeloupe in Mexico, to Czestekova in Poland, to Fatima in Portugal, to Lourdes in France and to the so-called holy house of Loreto. He went there to prepare for his visit to Ireland and in doing so appeared to endorse the fanciful legend that the house of Mary in Nazareth had been miraculously transported first to Dalmatia and then to Loreto.

Shrines and alleged appearances of Mary

The other shrines mentioned have a similar background. In Lourdes it was the fourteen-year-old Bernadette Soubirois who saw what was invisible to others, a vision of Mary with her message: 'I am the immaculate conception' — the dogma declaring this to be true had been formulated only four years earlier. In 1846 a boy and a girl had a similar vision at La Salette near Grenobles in France. In Fatima it was three illiterate children aged ten to thirteen who saw the vision of a lady who declared herself to be 'Our Lady of the Rosary'. In Knock, a remote village in Co. Mayo in the west of Ireland, it was a group of country folk who saw a vision on the church wall illuminated by a brilliant light. Although they were kneeling in the pouring rain, very conveniently no rain fell on the gable wall of the parish church![7] In every case the outcome was notoriety, followed by floods of pilgrims visiting the shrines to pray and also, incidentally, to assimilate more of the atmosphere of Marian devotion.

Rome has officially taken a somewhat ambivalent stand on the question of whether these 'apparitions' actually took place. Thus in 1877 the Congregation of Rites made a statement on the apparitions at Lourdes and La Salette: 'Such apparitions are neither approved nor condemned by the Holy See. They are simply authorized as pious beliefs based on purely human faith or evidence.' So at the request of a bishop the Vatican may grant liturgical or other privileges to the shrine and it may even encourage the devotion of pilgrimage connected with the apparition ... but in granting such approval it does not guarantee the historical fact of the apparition.'

I had an interesting commentary on this ambiguous attitude just a few days before writing this chapter. There was a television programme[8] centred on Grangecon, a tiny village in Co. Wicklow. The postmistress was a zealous devotee of the cult of Mary. She had a statuette in a glass-fronted case which was clearly an object of regular devotion. She claimed that tears had appeared from the eyes of the image. Her conviction was that Mary was grieving and clearly had a message to pass on. Already the devotees began to arrive, though in modern Ireland the visitors also included the curious and the cynical.

The local priest, while not condemning the devotion if it helped the adherents, had a more rational explanation. He pointed out that the eyes of the image were held in place by glue which could react to a rise in temperature by melting and producing tears! It was a good illustration of the policy established in 1877 — if you are credulous you may believe it all as long as it deepens your piety, but if you are critical you may dismiss it as a delusion! Some may call this pastoral advice while others might justifiably call it cynicism.

John Paul, however, is not among the critics of Knock or Fatima but is the leader of the enthusiastic adherents. In any case his beliefs about Mary are rooted much more deeply than in any emotional stirring he may have experienced in his pilgrimages. He holds them because he so completely accepts the dogmatic teaching of the Roman Catholic Church. He and great numbers like him did not become devotees of Mary because of these legendary appearances — though he would not dismiss them as such — but rather because he had been steeped in the Marian teaching and the liturgical practices which stemmed from it. To that teaching we must now turn.

The immaculate conception

The starting-point for our consideration of the development of Marian piety must be the promulgation of the dogma of the immaculate conception of Mary. The pope was Pius IX, who was later to force through a reluctant Vatican Council the dogma of papal infallibility. Pius was fully persuaded of his own infallible teaching well before the Vatican Council. He therefore presented the theory of the immaculate conception not as an optional extra but as an obligatory requirement. So he added a solemn postscript: 'If therefore, any person shall dare to think — which God forbid — otherwise than has been defined by us, let them clearly know that they stand condemned by their own judgement, that they have made shipwreck of their faith and fallen from the unity of the church.'

The word 'immaculate' is derived from the Latin word *'macula'* which means 'a stain, blemish, or spot'. It needs to be emphasized that this has nothing to do with the biblical truth of the virgin birth, where the one who was conceived without spot or blemish was our Lord Jesus. The papal theory refers rather to the moment when Mary herself was conceived, and claims that she was faultless. This claim implies that Mary shared the sinlessness of Christ.

The obvious reply to such a fanciful notion is the clear admission of sin by Mary herself in her song of praise recorded in Luke 1:46-55: 'My soul magnifies the Lord, and my spirit rejoices in God my Saviour.' In this song she reflects the theme which is so often on the lips of Christians as we thank the Lord who has saved us from our sins by sending his own Son to bear our sins in his own body on the tree (1 Peter 2:24). The significance of the word 'Saviour' is seen in its verbal form in Matthew 1:21: 'He will save his people from their sins.' So in praising her Saviour Mary is rejoicing that she is a sinner saved by grace. She marvels that, sinner though she is, God has given her the humbling privilege of being the human agent for the incarnation of the Son of God.

Rome, however, has an answer to this objection. It was first formulated by Duns Scotus (1266-1308), who advanced the speculative notion of 'redemption by exemption'. This enabled him to say that yes, Mary had a Saviour and yes, she was redeemed. Her redemption, however, was different from ours in that we are redeemed from the guilt and penalty of our sins, whereas she was delivered from contracting sin and thus can be presented as being conceived in an immaculate or sinless condition.

This fanciful theory conflicts with the entire biblical testimony on the nature of redemption. The word can only be understood against the background of slavery, which is why it was applied to the deliverance of Israel from Egypt. For the same reason it was a word easily understood in the first century A.D. when a slave was set free after the redemption price had been paid. So we were redeemed, 'not with perishable things such as silver or gold ... but with the precious blood of Christ' (1 Peter 1:18-19). This shows the absurdity of Duns Scotus' theory since according to him the price was paid to deliver from a slavery which never existed and the blood was shed to cleanse a non-existent stain.

Always a virgin?

Allied to this false idea of her immaculate conception is the theory of Mary's perpetual virginity, namely that she remained always a virgin. This is plainly contradicted by the record of Joseph's reaction to the angel's message reassuring him as to Mary's chastity: 'He took [Mary as] his wife, but knew her not until she had borne a son' (Matt. 1:24-25). The key word is 'until', which obviously refers to a point of time when a course of action which has been suspended is resumed — in this case Joseph deferred intimacy with Mary until the baby was born. Ronald Knox, a famous convert to Rome, perpetrated a gross mistranslation in his version of the New Testament when he substituted 'when' for 'until' — and then had the gall to add a footnote acknowledging that the word meant 'until'! One might for example, speak of an engaged couple today going against the pattern of so many friends, and refusing to sleep together until they were married. It would import a different and absurd meaning if their 'until' was changed to 'when'.

We have no need then to engage in the spurious theories which try to find a mother to whom the brothers and sisters of Jesus, described as such in the Gospels, really belonged. They belonged obviously to Mary, the mother of Jesus. He was her first-born and to deny that is to insult God the Creator's sanctifying the physical union between a man and his wife. Mary was a virgin when she conceived but that condition ceased when she and Joseph came together to produce a family.

Sinlessness ascribed to Mary

Even more seriously erroneous is the totally unbiblical assertion that Mary was to the end of her days totally without sin. 'By the grace of God Mary remained free of every personal sin her whole life long.'[9] So she is designated 'the All Holy'. The claim is made that she had the 'splendour of an entirely unique holiness'. This flies in the face of the vigorous assertion by Paul that 'None is righteous, no not one ... since all have sinned and fall short of the glory of God' (Rom 3:10,23). He did not make an exception for Mary!

The catechism tries to justify its fanciful claims by appealing to Ephesians 1:3-4, which affirms that all Christians have been blessed 'in Christ with every spiritual blessing'. Without the remotest scrap of evidence the catechism claims that Mary was even more blessed than the rest of us! What this special pleading does is to underline the fact that the word 'favoured' addressed to Mary in Luke 1:28 is applied to every believer in Ephesians 1:3 (the same word is used in both passages in the Greek). The word means that we are debtors to God's grace for every gift we have received and whatever responsibility has been given to us. We, like Mary, stand before the Lord as sinners forgiven by the grace of God and endowed by that same grace with the power of the Holy Spirit to do his will.

To apply Ephesians 1:3 to Mary to a pre-eminent degree is also to bring her under the indictment of the second chapter of the epistle. There Paul reminded the church in Ephesus and thus the individual believers: 'And ...' — the 'and' indicates that the people he addressed were still the same ones as he addressed in 1:3,6 — 'And you he made alive, when you were dead through the trespasses and sins in which you once walked, following the course of this world' (Eph. 2:1). Lest any might feel they were not among the 'sons of disobedience' Paul added, and included himself, 'Among these we all once lived.' So every Christian, including Mary, started in that condition and continued in it until saved by grace. The true Mary would have found no difficulty here as she rejoiced as a sinner in God her Saviour.

Rome, however, goes even further in elevating Mary to a key rôle in the work of salvation. Having been raised to the same level of sinlessness as the Saviour, she is given a share in the atonement. Thus while the Gospels picture her as a grief-stricken mother seeing her son die, Rome sees her as 'joining herself with his sacrifice in her mother's heart'.[10] The Bible says that God gave his only begotten Son but Rome involves Mary in that giving of the Saviour. It is no surprise to discover the conclusion that one of the titles given to her is 'mediatrix', i.e. female mediator, in utter defiance of the assertion of Paul that 'There is one mediator' (1 Tim. 2:5).

The assumption

Pius XII added further to the accumulation of false doctrine undergirding the cult of Mary. In 1950 he issued another dogma declaring that she had been given the privilege 'like her Son before her to conquer death ... and to be raised body and soul to the glory of heaven, to shine refulgent as Queen at the right hand of her Son'. Lest any should imagine that this is an optional extra — 'I'm a Catholic but I don't really accept this' — Pius added a solemn postscript. 'Wherefore, if anyone — which God forbid — should wilfully dare to deny or call in doubt what has been defined by us, let him know that he certainly has abandoned the divine and Catholic faith.'

Search the New Testament from end to end and there is not the remotest hint of this teaching. In contrast the resurrection of Jesus was prophesied beforehand both in the Old Testament and in the repeated statements of Jesus himself. The event was declared and the evidence adduced. Paul could list the great number of personal witnesses. That is why we are so persuaded that Jesus truly conquered death and rose again. But where are the prophecies about Mary's assumption? Where are the witnesses to this event? The answer is a profound and significant silence. Apart from a reference to Mary's presence with many others in the post-ascension gathering, she disappears completely from the pages of the New Testament. Here were the documents which were basic to the apostolic testimony. Here was guidance to the new-born churches as to their pattern of worship and their way of life. But in utter contrast to the excessive claims about Mary in Roman Catholic statements and writing, the New Testament is totally silent.

A rôle in the work of salvation?

In view of so many departures from biblical teaching, it is not surprising to find that the descent into error became even more pronounced. The Second Vatican Council, lauded by many outsiders as if it was the herald of a new day, only succeeded in deepening the darkness. So Mary is presented as one who had a unique rôle in the work of salvation, not simply, as she is seen in the Gospels, as the virgin mother of the Saviour, but as one who was jointly involved with Christ himself in the accomplishment of his work — 'co-operating in the work of salvation.'[11]

In support of such claims there is a serious misuse of Scripture which yields wholly erroneous conclusions. For example, the record of the first miracle at Cana recorded by John (John 2:1-11) is used to encourage the false notion that the intercession of Mary has special power. This interpretation ignores the fact that Jesus gently but firmly rebuked Mary. A note in the Roman Catholic edition of the RSV does admit that his words, 'O woman what have you to do with me?' are an expression which 'always implies a divergence of view'. The note goes on to claim, without any supporting evidence, that this divergence was neither 'an unqualified refusal, still less a rebuke'. However, one thing is certain: his reply most assuredly is *not* an endorsement of the rôle of Mary as an intercessor with special power! Jesus makes it abundantly clear by his expressed 'divergence of view' that he saw things very differently from Mary!

Appeal is also made to Mark's account, but here again the text (Mark 3:31-35) points to a totally different conclusion from that reached in the Vatican document. Mark recorded how the mother and brothers of Jesus came to the house where he was teaching. His hearers told him, 'Your mother and your brothers are outside, asking for you.' Here, surely, was an occasion for extolling Mary; yet Jesus gave no such eulogy. Instead he replied with a question: 'Who are my mother and my brothers?' The obvious answer was to point to the new arrivals outside. Jesus totally disagreed. Mark made this very clear as he described Jesus' action and words: 'Looking around on those who sat about him, he said, "Here are my mother and my brothers! Whoever does the will of God is my brother, and sister and mother."' So while Mary's rôle in conceiving the Messiah was unique, her status before God was exactly the same as that of any disciple. It was not the physical relationship that mattered so much as the faith of the believers. Such faith put the humblest disciple on a par with Mary, who shared the same salvation on the same terms.

Even more devastating to false claims for Mary is the passage in Luke's Gospel to which the council document also appeals (Luke 11:27-28). Luke described the sudden interruption of Jesus' public discourse. A woman was obviously moved to the depths and 'raised her voice and said to him, "Blessed is the womb that bore you, and the breasts that you sucked!"' If those had remained the only words Luke recorded they would have been a powerful argument for the use of the rosary! However, moved by the Spirit, he went on to give Jesus' reply. It was a complete contradiction of what the woman had asserted. His reply could not have been more forthright: 'Blessed rather are those who hear the word of God and keep it!' The key word here is 'rather'. The Greek word thus translated is used in an answer to correct an earlier statement. So it might be translated as 'on the contrary'.[12] Could any statement be clearer? Mary's blessedness was not due to some special rôle. What made her blessed was precisely the same as that which makes every Christian equally blessed, namely receiving and keeping the Word of God.

Mother of the church?

With all this opposing evidence it is a feeble argument to try to change the apostle John's record into a supposed endorsement of the Vatican Council's claim that Mary is the mother of the church.[13] The appeal is to the moment when Jesus spoke from the cross to his mother: '"Woman, behold your son!"'

Then he said to the disciple, "Behold your mother!"' (John 19:26-27). Was this Jesus committing his church to the care of his mother? John certainly didn't see it that way. He knew that Mary would need much help in facing her grief. The total silence about Joseph suggests that she was now a widow. The earlier refusal of the brothers of Jesus to accept him pointed to an inability on their part to sympathize adequately with a grieving and traumatized woman. Jesus, who took our nature in its fulness, had the tender affection of any son for his mother and the concern for her future welfare. John's response showed how he understood it. It was certainly not some new worshipping relationship with Mary: 'And from that hour the disciple took her to his own home' (John 19:27). It is a far cry from this picture of the tenderness of Jesus to the unsubstantiated speculation that Mary as 'mother of the church' has a ministry of intercession in heaven by which 'she continues to win for us gifts of eternal salvation'.

The development did not end with Vatican II. Paul VI, in his *Marialis Cultus*, issued in February 1974, encouraged strongly the devotion to Mary. He tried, as Rome has traditionally done, to distinguish between the worship given to God alone *(latria)*, the adoration of Mary *(hyperdulia)* and the veneration of the saints *(dulia)*. This distinction is totally without biblical warrant, and in practice is virtually impossible to sustain. The extravagant devotion to Mary, with the ascription to her of all kinds of elaborate titles, is simply idolatrous. But lest anyone should query the excessive repetition in the Rosary of appeals to Mary to pray for us, we are assured by Paul VI that the practice has been 'approved by papal authority, which also enriched it with numerous indulgences'.[14] There in fact is the essential character of the cult of Mary — it is the invention of the popes rather than the witness of the biblical writers!

Tradition and the cult of the goddess

One must surely ask, how did such a pagan cult infiltrate the Christian church? The answer lies in the paganizing of the churches after the fourth-century *rapprochement* with the state in the reign of the Emperor Constantine. This is not to say that heresies were not already present — the father of lies saw to it that they were! Rather, it was the era when the floodgates began to be opened and so many of the developing errors of the Middle Ages can be traced to that period. This is eminently true of the cult of Mary, the roots of which can be found in the cult of the Mother Goddess so popular in the fourth century. As we noted earlier, the very titles of the goddess used then, 'Our Lady' and *'Stella Maris'*, have been adopted. The picture of Isis and Horus, the Mother Goddess with the child on her knee, has been repeated innumerable times in the picture of the madonna and the infant Jesus. It is noteworthy that the cult developed in its early days in those centres where the devotion to the Mother Goddess was established. Egypt was the centre of the worship of Isis. Ephesus had long been associated with the worship of Artemis — witness the riot recorded by Luke (Acts 19:23-41) when the enraged devotees of the goddess erupted in fury against Paul's preaching, with its exclusive claims for Christ. Another important centre was Phrygia, where the great mother Cybele was the focus of devotion.

The cult had even earlier roots, as we discover in the denunciations of Jeremiah (Jer. 7:18-20; 44:17,25). God's judgement was pronounced on the devotees of the 'queen of heaven' — another title which has come down the centuries. This deity has older Canaanite roots in the cult of Ashtoreth, or Astarte (1 Kings 11:5). One can understand the popular appeal of these ancient cults with their emphasis on the motherly care of the goddess. This concept has percolated into popular Catholic piety and into the kind of argument used by

Catholic apologists. Who, they will ask, could be more sym-
pathetic than a mother, and who could have greater influence
with her son? The answer to that is to turn to the letter to the
Hebrews, where Jesus is presented as the all-sympathetic High
Priest (Heb. 4:15). There is no need of the alleged sympathy
of Mary when we have direct access to the Lord himself.

Let me end by emphasizing as strongly as possible that this
'Mary' of Catholic devotion has no links whatever with Mary
of Nazareth. The latter was a humble believer entrusted with
the unique privilege of conceiving the incarnate Son of God.
We thank God for her, just as we do for Joseph or Peter or Paul,
or any of the believers in the New Testament whose faith and
obedience encourage or challenge us. The Babylonian goddess with her pretensions is a hollow sham. Mary, the mother
of Jesus, learnt how to recede so completely into the background that she disappears in the pages of the New Testament.
But then her aim was what ours should be — that the one and
only mediator, our Lord Jesus Christ, should have all the glory.

The 'Mary' of Catholic theology and devotion embodies
perfectly their doctrine of merit. 'From this community of will
and suffering between Christ and Mary she merited to become
the restorer of the world and the dispenser of all the benefits
which Jesus won for us by his death'[15] — that was Pius X
ignoring the truth that Jesus himself bore our sins, and the
further truth that the Holy Spirit is the dispenser of gospel
blessings. This doctrine of merit embodied in 'Mary' indicates
the basic reason for Rome's resistance to the doctrine of
justification by faith alone through grace alone. Much as they
may protest that Mary is still human, the fact remains that the
rôle they have given her, the extravagant titles (Advocate,
Helper, Benefactress and Mediatrix), the omniscience required to know the prayers of people around the world — all
this points to the ultimate idolatry, and the enthroning of a
female goddess alongside the Saviour.

9.
Why priests?

The chapter heading will be familiar to anyone who has read Hans Küng's short book on the subject. His arguments did not convince the Vatican any more than did the theme of his other book the title of which was also in the form of a question, *Infallible?* Indeed he forfeited his position as an officially recognized Roman Catholic teacher. Yet surely Küng was being biblical, as he certainly was not in some other major books, when he maintained: 'In contradistinction to the pagan or Jewish cult a Christian does not need the mediation of a priest to enter the innermost sanctuary of his temple, that is to reach God himself.'[1] His blunt statement, 'All believers are priests,'[2] echoes the passionate affirmation of the leaders of the Protestant Reformation.

The Vatican Catechism, however, clings to the notion of a special priesthood. It admits that there is a common priesthood, but claims that the special priestly ministry of the ordained clerics is necessary for the fulfilment of this common priesthood. The catechism bases this claim on tradition and adds, 'not without a basis in sacred Scripture'.[3] The alleged biblical justification is given in a footnote which refers to Hebrews 5:6 and 7:11. But this is to twist Scripture, for the verses quoted quite explicitly refer to the unique ministry of Jesus Christ himself, the great High Priest.

Christ the High Priest

Those misquoted references serve as a reminder that it is the epistle to the Hebrews which gives the final answer to any notion of a priestly caste. The constant emphasis is on the pre-eminence of Christ. He is the final Prophet to whom the Old Testament prophets pointed. He is supreme above the angels, who minister to the believers but are not to be invoked. His ministry is the consummation of the law of Moses, who was God's faithful servant while Jesus is God's only begotten Son. Finally, his priesthood fulfilled and superseded that of the Levites.

The Levites had a ministry whose authorization was from God. Of necessity it was a transitory ministry in that the Old Testament priests had their own sins which needed atonement. At the same time they were mortal, so that death removed one generation and ushered in the next. Jesus, however, is revealed as the final and supreme High Priest. He is the eternal priest with 'neither beginning of days nor end of life' (Heb. 7:3). 'He holds his priesthood permanently' (Heb. 7:24). His birth within the tribe of Judah marked him as distinct from the descendants of Levi. His priesthood was not tarnished as theirs was by sin. So he had no need to atone for his own sins, but was fully available to atone for ours. Thus, 'We ... have such a high priest, holy, blameless, unstained, separated from sinners, exalted above the heavens' (Heb. 7:26).

To speak of a priest is to speak of offerings. The Levitical priests offered on behalf of the people of God the whole range of Levitical sacrifices — sin offerings, burnt offerings, thank offerings and fellowship offerings. Yet in all the sacrificial system there was a fatal flaw which called for divine remedial action. That flaw is summed up in Hebrews: 'It is impossible that the blood of bulls and goats should take away sins' (Heb. 10:4). Their sacrifice was only a foreshadowing of the perfect sacrifice yet to come. Christ's is the perfect sacrifice for his death meant 'the offering of the body of Jesus Christ once for all' (Heb. 10:10).

There is a further underlying theme which has especial relevance in face of Rome's claim that the priest at the altar continues to offer 'the holy sacrifice of the mass'. That theme has been summarized in the phrase, 'the finished work of Christ'. Roman apologists speak of an eternal self-offering by Jesus in heaven, with the priest at the altar leading the people of God into a participation in that sacrifice. However, the emphasis in Hebrews rejects such a notion. Lying behind the theory is an attempt to reconcile the truth of Jesus' perfect offering and the oft-repeated masses. So Rome would claim that the mass is not another sacrifice but simply a sharing in the continuing offering in heaven.

Hebrews totally rebuts this argument. The picture it presents is not that of a priest in the heavenly temple before an altar. Rather it presents the Christ who 'when he had made purification for sins ... sat down at the right hand of the Majesty on high' (1:3). We sit down when we have completed a task. We may take a break in some major task, but when it is thoroughly complete we sit down in thankfulness that we have been able to finish the work. So the picture of the seated Christ recurs in the epistle: 'And every priest stands daily at his service, offering repeatedly the same sacrifices, which can never take away sins. But when Christ had offered for all time a single sacrifice for sins, he sat down at the right hand of God' (Heb. 10:11-12).

This stress on the once-for-all nature of Jesus' sacrifice is further emphasised by the use of two Greek adverbs, *hapax* and *ephapax*, the latter being an intensification of the former. So the firm 'once' is underlined by the more insistent 'once for all'. It is as if grammar is being utilized to give the most complete statement possible of the finality of the sacrifice at Calvary. In Hebrews 10:26-27 the point is reinforced by the use of our death as an analogy. It is obviously once for all and so also Christ was offered once as a never-to-be-repeated sacrifice.

The apostle Peter uses the same adverb to emphasize that 'Christ ... died for sins once for all' (1 Peter 3:18). The stronger adverb is employed to hammer home the point. Christ offered his sacrifice 'once for all' (Heb. 7:27). 'He entered once for all into the Holy Place' (Heb. 9:12). His offering of his body was once for all (Heb. 10:10). Paul used the same adverb with the same emphasis in his epistle to the Romans: 'The death he died he died to sin, once for all' (Rom. 6:10).

The obvious conclusion to draw from this wide range of apostolic testimony is that there is no longer a priestly caste as there was in the preparatory covenant when the Levites exercised their priestly office. Furthermore one must conclude that the final atoning sacrifice has been offered and accepted. To speak of a continuing self-offering, and of an earthly priest offering such an atoning offering, is to face the rebuttal of the seated Christ whose work has been finished. It is also to meet the rejection by the Father who has accepted once for all the perfect sacrifice presented at the heavenly mercy-seat. It is not God who needs to be propitiated by a continuing offering on an earthly altar. It is we who need to be reminded of what has already been decisively wrought by Christ and equally decisively accepted by the Father.

Of course it is true that the sacrificial language of the Levitical ritual is used in the New Testament to describe the offering we bring. But one thing which is abundantly clear is that never is there any hint of a propitiatory offering — there is no equivalent to the sin offering (Lev. 4:21; 5:15) since Christ has offered that once for all. There is, however, room for our response to that once-for-all sacrifice. There is thus a place for the thank-offering. So Paul uses the language of Old Testament sacrifice, but clearly without any trace of blood-shedding or atonement: 'I appeal to you therefore, brethren, by the mercies of God, to present your bodies as a living sacrifice, holy and acceptable to God, which is your spiritual worship' (Rom. 12:1). Here is the logic of holiness — hence his 'therefore'. It is in view of all that God has done and in view of his mercies that we respond in self-offering. Our self-offering is in no sense an attempt to win God's favour. That has been already granted through Christ. Rather it is the glad response of our hearts as we show our thanks 'not only with our lips but in our lives'.[4]

The same responsive note is seen in the teaching on almsgiving, which again is viewed not as a duty, and emphatically not as a way of gaining favour, but rather as the grateful response of one who feels indebted to the free grace of God. So the apostle rejoiced in the response of Macedonia, 'For in a severe test of affliction, their abundance of joy and their extreme poverty have overflowed in a wealth of liberality on their part' (2 Cor. 8:2). He further designates this kind of giving as 'service' — the Greek word used is *leitoupgia*, which comes across in the English liturgy which speaks of an act of worship. In agreement with this emphasis we find both our songs of praise and our giving to meet the needs of others described as sacrifices: 'Through him then let us continually offer up a sacrifice of praise to God, that is, the fruit of lips that acknowledge his name. Do not neglect to do good and to share what you have, for such sacrifices are pleasing to God' (Heb. 13:15-16). To use a bald literalism and call praise actual sacrifice would be as absurd as to say that the fruit of our lips implies that we sing with an apple or pear in our mouths!

Sacraments

In dealing with the unique priestly ministry of Christ we have inevitably impinged on a discussion of the sacraments, so it is time to concentrate more directly on this issue. First of all, it may be of help to discuss the actual word 'sacrament'. The original Latin word *'sacramentum'* was familiar in the legions of the Roman Empire as it referred to the oath of loyalty given by the soldier at his enrolment. It is not surprising that the early generations of Christians found it a convenient word to describe two ordinances in which there was a strong notion of commitment. So the new convert declared his allegiance to his Saviour in his baptism. Similarly, the Lord's Supper was seen as a renewal of that initial commitment. There were, of course, many other aspects of truth displayed in these two visible ordinances, but the notion of commitment was always prominent.

Because the term was in itself neutral the Protestant Reformers found no difficulty in using the word in its original sense. As Roman Catholic sacramental teaching has continued to develop, there is much more reluctance among evangelicals to use the term because of the associations with what are viewed as unbiblical emphases. Certainly the word 'ordinance', which would be more common among the free churches, stresses an important point — namely that the sacraments have been ordained by the head of the church, Jesus Christ himself. He it was who instituted the Lord's Supper on the night of his betrayal with the accompanying command: 'Do this in remembrance of me... Do this, as often as you drink it [the cup], in remembrance of me' (1 Cor. 11:24-25). Baptism also was clearly ordained by Jesus Christ. When he gave his disciples their marching orders in the Great Commission, he gave instructions: 'Go therefore and make disciples of all nations, baptizing them in the name of the Father and of the Son and of the Holy Spirit' (Matt. 28:19).

Rome, however, claims that there are seven sacraments. Hans Küng firmly dismissed this idea of the seven sacraments as 'a product of history unknown during the first thousand years, present for the first time in the twelfth century'.[5] The

Vatican Catechism, however, still continues to go beyond the clear evidence of Scripture. In addition to the two sacraments which, all agree, were ordained by Christ, there are additions: marriage, confirmation, ordination, penance and extreme unction *(unctio in extremis)*.

If we begin with *marriage* it is clear that this was not ordained by the incarnate Son since it was first laid down at the creation of Adam and Eve. When Jesus was questioned on the issue of divorce he replied by pointing them back to the narrative in Genesis: 'Have you not read that he who made them from the beginning made them male and female, and said, "For this reason a man shall leave his father and mother and be joined to his wife, and the two shall become one flesh"?' (Matt. 19:4-5). So Jesus' endorsement of the sanctity of marriage was in fact simply an echo of the original revelation. Marriage is a creation ordinance, not like baptism and the Lord's Supper, which are ordinances of the gospel. The requirements of marriage are not simply for Christians since the Creator described them as obligatory from the very dawn of human history.

In the practice of *confirmation* there simply is no clear word from Jesus on the subject. We may point directly to Scripture for quite explicit statements by Jesus laying down the requirements for the two great gospel ordinances, but nowhere is he recorded as having enjoined confirmation by a bishop — but then elsewhere we have noted that elder and bishop are interchangeable terms in the New Testament! The introduction of the christening of infants in the fourth century led to a requirement for some form of personal affirmation by the Christian who had been christened in unconscious infancy. But of an institution enacted by Jesus there is no evidence.

The laying-on of hands was, of course, recorded in the New Testament, as indeed it was also in the Old Testament. In both covenants it was used as a visible token of invoking God's blessing. So a father might lay hands on his son in the way that Jacob laid his hands on his two grandsons (Gen. 48:14). It was also used as an act of commissioning as, for example, in the case of Joshua, who was set apart by Moses, not to the priesthood, but to be ruler of Israel (Num. 27:23). The commissioning of the seven men appointed to oversee the distribution of alms was also accompanied by the laying on of hands (Acts 6:6).

The invocation of God's blessing was also reflected in Jesus' action as 'He laid his hands upon a few sick people and healed them' (Mark 6:5). Later he did it on a wider scale when many came and 'He laid his hands on every one of them and healed them' (Luke 4:40). It could also be used as a token of fellowship. Thus the apostles indicated that the once-hated Samaritans were accepted by what had hitherto been almost completely a Jewish church. The indication of this acceptance was the laying-on of hands, just as later Paul showed his acceptance of the former disciples of John the Baptist in the same way (Acts 8:17; 19:6). It was also employed when Timothy was set apart for the ministry of the Word (1 Tim. 4:14). Paul and Barnabas, already experienced preachers, had hands laid on them to commission them for a new phase in their ministry as they were sent by the church in Antioch on their first missionary journey.

This variety of usage would seem to preclude the narrowing of the laying-on of hands to a very small range of people. Even more does it shut out the idea that this was a sacramental sign ordained by Christ, whether for the ordination of ministers, or the confirming of recently converted Christians. There simply is no record in the four Gospels of Jesus giving these alleged sacraments to his church, whereas, let me stress again, there is firm and explicit evidence of baptism and the Lord's Supper being thus instituted.

The claims that penance and extreme unction are sacraments will be dealt with in a later chapter. At this point it seems appropriate to look more closely at the nature of a sacrament with special reference to the two gospel sacraments, baptism and the Lord's Supper. The Vatican Catechism sets out Rome's teaching: 'The sacraments are perceptible signs (words and actions) accessible to our human nature. By the action of Christ and the power of the Holy Spirit they make present efficaciously the grace that they signify.'[6] If any reader is uncertain as to the meaning of 'efficaciously', the catechism spells it out more specifically: 'Celebrated worthily in faith, the sacraments confer the grace that they signify. They are efficacious because in them Christ himself is at work.'[7] In other words, the sacraments, it is claimed, actually effect what they represent: 'They communicate the grace that each sacrament signifies.'

In making these statements the catechism is simply echoing the decrees of the Council of Trent. So the claim is clearly made: 'The sacraments act *ex opere operato*' (literally: 'by the very fact of the action's being performed').[8] This affirmation is carried to its logical conclusion: 'The Church affirms that for believers the sacraments of the New Covenant are necessary for salvation.'[9] This latter assertion explains the desperate urgency to christen a new-born baby who is clearly going to die. There are shades here of the medieval notion of the *limbus infantorum* reserved for infants who have died without baptism and who, while not suffering the pains of hell, are denied the vision of God which is the supreme blessing of heaven.

The Second Vatican Council left out the phrase *'ex opere operato'* in the constitution on the sacred liturgy. This seems to have been a concession. Thus Neuner and Dupuis, in *The Christian Faith*, commented on the avoidance of the controversial phrase, claiming that the constitution emphasized instead the presence of Christ. The catechism, however, returns to the traditional formula, and thus to the notion that the sacraments are channels through which the grace of God flows. So baptism is presented as not only signifying the washing of regeneration and renewal by the Holy Spirit, but as the effective means to achieve these: 'For it signifies and actually brings about the birth of water and the Spirit'.[10]

Rome insists on three essentials for a valid sacrament: first, the matter (water and bread and wine); secondly, the form (the baptismal formula and the words of institution); and, thirdly, the intention to do what the church intends. I pointed out in the historical survey that generations of degenerate popes in the Middle Ages pose a large query about their intentions. The same query must be registered in the case of the thousands of priests who have left the priesthood. Can one be sure that before their final decisive exit they all continued to exercise the right intention? The uncertainty about the validity of any sacrament was highlighted, not by a hostile critic, but by the renowned sixteenth-century Cardinal Bellarmine, an outstanding exponent of the teaching of the Council of Trent and the personal theologian of the pope. He wrote, 'No one can be certain with the certainty of faith that he has a true sacrament, since the sacrament is not formed without the intention of the minister, and no one can see the intention of another.'[11]

To move from the shifting sands of sacramental validity is to discover in the New Testament a totally different emphasis and an accompanying assurance. There the two great gospel ordinances are seen as, to quote Augustine's helpful analogy, 'visible words'. They present in visual form to eyes, mouth and body the basic themes of burial with Christ and rising to new life, and the assurance coming from the finished work of Christ celebrated in bread and wine. There is, however, in the Scriptures a vitally important element if we are to find blessing in the visible words — that element is faith.

With Rome faith has been moved from its central position as the response of the believer to the gracious initiative of God. The catechism indeed speaks of the sacraments of faith and claims: 'Celebrated worthily in faith, the sacraments confer the grace that they signify.'[12] One might ask about the response of faith in an unconscious infant, or in a dying man in a coma to whom 'the last rites' are administered.

Rome's answer is that 'The Church's faith precedes the faith of the believer.' That means that great numbers were thus regenerated, in Rome's view, who yet never gave the slightest indications of any remote interest in the gospel for the rest of their lives. It means also that a man who has lived in contempt for God and rejection of Christ may yet, in his unconscious state, be prepared for glory without once having shown any sign of repentance. One is forced to say that the so-called 'faith of the church' seems much more like wishful thinking. True faith, as the apostle Paul pointed out, is not some vague quality. Rather, 'Faith comes from what is heard, and what is heard comes by the preaching of Christ' (Rom. 10:17). The Bible knows nothing of a vicarious faith where a representative responds to God's grace on our behalf. 'So each of us shall give account of himself to God' (Rom. 14:12).

On the one side we meet the deep uncertainties of the sacramental approach. We are left wondering about the intention of the priest, or of the bishop who ordained him, or of the priest who originally christened that bishop. It becomes a series of questions to which the only answer seems to be a very tentative hopefulness. By contrast the New Testament speaks with a sure note: 'When we cry "Abba Father!" it is the Spirit himself bearing witness with our spirit that we are children of God (Rom. 8:15-16). John's aim in writing his epistle was that we might be sure: 'I write this to you who believe in the name of the Son of God, that you may know that you have eternal life' (1 John 5:13).

Such assurance comes from the objective truths revealed in the promises of Scripture, and also from the evidence in our own hearts of the assuring voice of the Spirit. Instead of trying in vain to assess the intentions of the line of priests who have ministered sacramentally, the seeker is pointed rather to the sure words of the gospel, and to the evidence in our hearts that we are born of God. We turn, not to some earthly priest, but to the great High Priest, Jesus the Son of God. We find one who is able to sympathize with our weaknesses since he himself 'in every respect has been tempted just as we are, yet without sin'. The assuring word immediately follows: 'Let us then with confidence draw near to the throne of grace, that we may receive mercy and find grace to help in time of need' (Heb. 4:14-16).

Baptism and the Lord's Supper are precious ordinances of Christ. Just as his audible word has sounded in our ears and in our hearts, so his visible words *(verba visibilia)* have thrust his grace and mercy into our face, into our mouth and all our senses. They thus become means whereby the promises are made so vivid to us that, as we respond in faith, baptism and the Lord's Supper reassure us. Our confidence is deepened, not into presumption but into joyful assurance.

10.
Penance and purgatory

The two most basic issues which confront all of us relate to sin and death. If I accept what God says in his word that 'All have sinned and fall short of the glory of God' (Rom. 3:23), then the cry of the jailer in Philippi provides me with an urgent and insistent question: 'What must I do to be saved?' (Acts 16:30). If I then accept a further word from God, 'It is appointed for men to die once, and after that comes judgement' (Heb. 9:27), then I am forced to ask how I may be ready to face death and judgement.

The most cursory glance at my own moral and spiritual frailty soon shows that I do not have the solution to my need of salvation in my own hands. Too easily I make resolves which are then broken. Too readily I give way to temptation. Too often the weakness of the flesh far outstrips the willingness of the spirit.

If in addition to all this I reflect on the fragility of life — how an accident or a heart attack can suddenly end it all — then the issue of death and judgement ceases to be a debating matter for theologians. It becomes the issue of supreme concern which makes every other major problem totally secondary. Jesus put it so succinctly as he pointed to the futility of so many of our discussions and our anxious concern: 'What does it profit a man, to gain the whole world and forfeit his life? For what can a man give in return for his life?' (Mark 8:36-37).

The Bible takes sin and death seriously, and necessarily so, since it is essentially a book about salvation. It is God's revelation of the divinely provided answer to the need of forgiveness. It also rings with assurance as it speaks of victory over death, and presents a firmly based hope for life beyond the grave.

The gospel, after all, is not good religious advice for those who are interested in moral self-improvement. Rather it is gloriously good news: 'The saying is sure and worthy of full acceptance, that Christ Jesus came into the world to save sinners' (1 Tim. 1:15). The addition of the brief personal application — 'and I am the foremost of sinners' — emphasizes that this is not a merely theoretical discussion. It reaches into the depths of individual need. It points to a personal enjoyment of this salvation, which is the essential element in facing death, not with presumption, but with divinely given confidence.

Sin is described in the Bible in many ways. It is disobedience to God. It is the rebellion of the creature against the Creator. It is a transgression of God's law, whether the law presented in the specific requirements of Scripture, or the law written on our hearts, where conscience is the judge appointed by God. It is also seen as turning aside from the path of righteousness so that the sinner is lost. It corrupts within so that, in Jeremiah's words, 'The heart is deceitful above all things, and desperately corrupt' (Jer. 17:9).

The persistence of the sinner in his folly is explained by Paul: 'The god of this world has blinded the minds of the unbelievers to keep them from seeing the light of the glory of Christ.' Lest the Christian should be tempted to self-congratulation for having seen the truth, Paul adds a corrective which gives all the glory to God: 'For it is the God who said, "Let light shine out of darkness," who has shone in our hearts to give the light of the knowledge of the glory of God in the face of Jesus Christ' (2 Cor. 4:4,6).

There is a wonderful simplicity in this good news. The complications and confusions which emerged later are not due to the unfolding of that original simplicity. Rather they are to be attributed to the emergence of false teaching which acts like rank weeds stifling a growing plant. So Paul reminds the Roman Christians that their response to his gospel was not an enrolment in some complex quest. The word is plain and clear: 'Do not say in your heart, "Who will ascend into heaven?" (that is, to bring Christ down) or "Who will descend into the abyss?" (that is, to bring Christ up from the dead). But what does it say? The word is near you, on your lips and in your heart (that is, the word of faith which we preach); because, if you confess with your lips that Jesus is Lord and believe in your heart that God raised him from the dead, you will be saved' (Rom. 10:6-9). How wonderful it would have been if the church in Rome, to which Paul wrote, had retained in subsequent generations a firm adherence to that simplicity! Instead Roman theologians have so modified and added to the simplicity of the gospel that deeply concerned seekers hear a very uncertain sound.

Mortal and venial sins

A major complication of the original revelation was the classification of sins. The distinction drawn is between venial and mortal sins. The word 'venial' comes from the Latin *venia* which means 'favour' or 'indulgence of faults'. Cicero linked it with *impunitas* — that is, freedom from punishment. So a venial sin is viewed as being less serious than a mortal sin. Venial sins are said to be 'everyday faults'.[1]

The Council of Trent made clear the distinction when it insisted that confession to a priest was essential for the pardon of mortal sins. Then the council affirmed that 'Venial sins, on the other hand, by which we are not excluded from the grace of God and into which we fall more frequently, though they may rightly and properly and without presumption be declared in confession, as the practice of pious people evinces, may nevertheless be omitted without guilt and can be expiated by many other remedies.'[2]

Mortal sins, which are also referred to in the catechism as 'grave', are clearly viewed as vastly more serious. Those who have fallen into grave sin 'have thus lost their baptismal grace'.[3] In other words they cease to love God: 'Mortal sin destroys charity [love] in the heart of man by a grave violation of God's law.'[4] Since the charity in the heart is in Rome's view the blessing which comes with baptism, when the stain of sin is removed and sanctifying grace imparted, there needs to be a fresh start so that penance is presented as a second bridge for those alienated from God.

Venial sins, by contrast, may weaken our love but do not set us in opposition to God. They do not break the covenant. Mortal sins, however, not only destroy our love now, but if the sinner dies in a state of mortal sin he goes neither to heaven nor to purgatory but to hell. So the catechism claims that venial sin is 'humanly reparable', for it 'does not deprive the sinner of sanctifying grace, friendship with God, charity and conse-quently eternal happiness'.[5] Mortal sin, on the other hand, can only be dealt with by confession and priestly absolution.

For a sin to be mortal there are three basic requirements. The object of mortal sin must be a 'grave matter' and it must be accompanied by 'full knowledge and deliberate consent'.[6] If we ask the meaning of a 'grave matter' the answer is that it is specified by the Ten Commandments, summarized as they are by Jesus in the twofold requirement to love God wholly and to love our neighbour as ourselves.

There is no scriptural justification for this cataloguing of sins. 1 John 5:16-17 is quoted, but in fact this passage contra-dicts both the claim that mortal sin may be cleansed through penance and the totally spurious notion that we can effect a change for someone who has already died. John holds out no hope and indeed insists that it is useless to pray for this kind of sin: 'I do not say that one is to pray for that.' Here is the kind of person who has deliberately, wilfully and decisively shut mind and heart against the truth. Far from being a backslider who will eventually return, this is the apostate who stubbornly goes on in his present state. It is the kind of abandoned attitude which Jesus described as sin against the Holy Spirit and which has no forgiveness. The reason surely is that a determined and persistent rejection of the Spirit's testimony to Christ hardens a sinner so that he ceases to hear the witness he has spurned.

The distinction between venial and mortal sins has serious implications. Any weakening of the gravity of sin is highly dangerous. To view some sins as being easily dealt with is to fail to appreciate how rigorously Scripture views all sin. When Jesus faced his rabbinic critics he pointed out that while murder and adultery are grievous in the sight of God, so also are the hidden sins of hate and lust, which in God's sight are equally foul.

All sin is an affront to God's holiness. For the Christian longing to grow in holiness sinful failure is always seen as ugly, since it harms our relationship with God. David discovered this anguish, as he disclosed in the great Psalms 32 and 51. As he poured out his heart to God, he recalled the months when he tried to quieten his conscience until finally the prophet Nathan exposed his sin. David's confession, however, went beyond admitting the wrong done to Bathsheba and her husband Uriah. What he had come to see was an even deeper truth; hence his cry: 'Against thee, thee only, have I sinned, and done that which is evil in thy sight' (Ps. 51:4). Such an awareness of sin as an affront to God could never reduce any sins to 'everyday faults'.

A true awareness of sin brings with it an urgent desire for forgiveness. Because we are not only ashamed before God but also feel the stain on our souls, we feel the need not only for repairing the breach in our relationship but also for an inner cleansing. Again and again the promises of the Word of God bring this pardon before us. There are many such promises, but one in particular seems to gather together the thoughts of pardon and also cleansing. John wrote so assuringly, 'If we confess our sins, he is faithful and just, and will forgive our sins and cleanse us from all unrighteousness' (1 John 1:9). If we ask how we should claim that promise, we are pointed directly to our great High Priest, our Supreme Pontiff, Jesus Christ: 'Let us then with confidence draw near to the throne of grace, that we may receive mercy' (Heb. 4:16).

Contrition and attrition

The simplicity of this approach to God is reflected in two words which are closely united in the Bible — repentance and faith. This simplicity, however, is plunged into complexity by Roman Catholic teaching which moves from different kinds of sin to different kinds of repentance. So after first having to decide whether the sins were venial or mortal the sinner has secondly to decide whether he should respond with contrition or attrition.

Contrition of heart consists of sorrow for sin committed and intention not to repeat the sin. This is intended to lead to confession to a priest and so to the hoped-for absolution. The Council of Trent, however, made provision for a lesser response which is described as attrition. This response is at a lower level and may be the product of the fear of hell. It requires penance in order to provide forgiveness, whereas a perfect act of contrition will lead to immediate pardon; but implicit in such an act of contrition is the intention to go to the confessional. So the higher or lower forms of repentance end at the same point — an appeal to what is termed the sacrament of penance. If anyone should object and claim that the fourteenth session of the Council of Trent is past history, it should be stressed again that tradition is still claimed to be one aspect of revelation. Certainly the catechism follows Trent and differentiates between contrition, which remits venial sins, and attrition, which it also calls 'contrition of fear'.[7]

Penance

Penance and anointing are linked together as 'the sacraments of healing', in that penance is seen as the remedy for the soul and anointing is provided for the sick in body. Penance is also called 'the sacrament of conversion' since it provides a way back for those who, having sinned after baptism, have forfeited baptismal grace and require healing for the soul. Further titles given to penance are the sacrament of confession, of forgiveness and of reconciliation. So it is viewed as a vitally important sacrament in the church's ministry. Indeed it is proclaimed as a 'second conversion' — baptism having been the first.

Yet in face of all this we find a total absence in the New Testament of the priest in the confessional — where, it must be noted, Rome views him, not as a counsellor to help troubled souls, but as the judicial representative of God the supreme Judge. Justification for such a rôle is sought in Jesus' commission to Peter, with the interpretation of the gift of the keys of the kingdom as being the authoritative appointment to judicial office.

This commission was given at Cæsarea Philippi, as recorded by Matthew (Matt. 16:19). It is important to note that two chapters later a similar authority is given(Matt. 18:15-18). This time, however, it is clear that it was not given only to the apostles. It comes in the context of Jesus' response to the problem, which arises so frequently in church life, where one brother has hurt another in some way and in spite of appeals in front of two or three witnesses and also to the church fellowship the offender refuses to make amends. The Lord's decision is that the impenitent one should be disciplined by the church and excluded from communion. Then follows the solemn reminder of the authority of the local assembly of God's people, even if they are only two or three in number.

There is a further application of the authority given by the Lord. It is seen in Peter's answer to his critics and later in his statement in the conference convened in Jerusalem. Peter recalled the wonderful privilege which God had given him of being a pioneer evangelist to the Gentiles. It was not a task he, as a Jew, had undertaken lightly. Indeed it required a revelation from heaven to overcome his stubborn Jewish prejudice and constrain him to go in response to the initiative of Cornelius. When he reached the centurion's house he simply presented the message of the gospel, and the Holy Spirit worked in Gentile hearts (Acts 10:34-43). He faced criticism but his critics ended by praising God that he had 'granted repentance unto life' (Acts 11:18).

Thus in the conference at Jerusalem Peter described what had happened as his discharge of a command to preach the gospel. Earlier the church in Jerusalem had rejoiced at news from Gentile Antioch that '[God] had opened a door of faith to the Gentiles' (Acts 14:28). So the authoritative discipline which closed the door which no one dare open (Matt. 18:18) is parallel to the opening of the door to the Gentiles (Acts 14:28). In neither case is there the remotest trace of a priestly or sacramental ministry. It is on one side the decision of a gathering in church fellowship, and on the other side a man preaching the gospel.

Rome may make a further appeal to the New Testament and quote from Jesus' words to his disciples after his resurrection:

'Receive the Holy Spirit. If you forgive the sins of any, they are forgiven; if you retain the sins of any, they are retained' (John 20:22-23). But it is not possible to construe this as an apostolic mandate. For one thing, the apostle Thomas was not there. More significantly, there were others present besides the apostles. In Luke's account we read of the women who had witnessed the resurrection meeting with the disciples. The gathering was further augmented by the arrival of the two disciples whom Jesus had met on the road to Emmaus. Thus this commission by the Lord was given to the whole fellowship. We are back to the pattern of Matthew 18, where the assembled church, rather than some priestly caste, is entrusted with the awesome task of godly discipline.

Penance also involves the teaching that while absolution is provided yet expiation or amends must be made. This does not refer to injuries done to others. Of course, where another person is involved, genuine repentance will lead the penitent to apologise to those he has hurt and to try to make reparations for grievous injury. However, the expiation which penance requires, when it speaks of making amends, refers rather to the sinner's relationship to God. Sin has been an affront to God's holiness and so, while the guilt of sin may be purged, there is the further need to make amends to God. Thus the priest claims not only the power to absolve the sinner from his guilt, but also the authority to be the arbiter who in his judicial rôle decides the amends which need to be made — that is, the penance to be carried out.

What makes this notion so seriously wrong is that it breaches the very basis of the gospel. Christ did not die to purchase a partial redemption. The forgiveness he purchased for us by his perfect sacrifice is total, and the purchase price does not require supplementing by any meritorious effort on our part. When he forgives there is no interest to pay because of continuing indebtedness to God. We have been ransomed 'not with perishable things such as silver or gold, but with the precious blood of Christ' (1 Peter 1:18-19). A demand for penance is an insult to God, both Father and Son. It impugns the righteousness of the Father, for it suggests that he requires an extra payment. It also insults the Saviour, since it implies that his offering was not sufficient. Toplady, the eighteenth-century hymn-writer, summed it up well in memorable lines:

> Payment God cannot twice demand,
> First at my bleeding Surety's hand,
> And then again at mine.

The glorious completeness of God's forgiveness is a theme for praise both in the Old Testament and in the New. When John writes that 'The blood of Jesus his Son cleanses us from all sin,' he is echoing the Psalms and the prophets as well as his fellow apostles. So the penitent's prayer is one of confident trust: 'Wash me, and I shall be whiter than snow' (Ps. 51:7). Isaiah has the same assuring promise, speaking as he does as the mouthpiece of the Lord: 'Though your sins are like scarlet, they shall be as white as snow' (Isa. 1:18). 'I have swept away your transgressions like a cloud and your sins like a mist' (Isa. 44:22).

Extreme unction

Rome presents penance as a sacrament of healing but the cure is sadly inadequate as human medication takes over from the heavenly Physician. What makes the notion of healing even stranger is the companion 'sacrament' of anointing. In spite of attempts to balance the matter, the fact remains that anointing has for a very long time been seen as being part of the last rites administered to the dying — it is *'unctio in extremis'*, usually known as extreme unction. The only mention of anything resembling such an anointing is in the epistle of James. But here the anointing is emphatically not a preparation for death, but points to a hoped-for recovery of health. So there is no hint that the one who calls for the elders, and is anointed, is on the point of death. On the contrary, the aim in view is clearly declared: 'The prayer of faith will save the sick man, and the Lord will raise him up' (James 5:15).

The other reference to which the apologist makes an appeal is the final words of Jesus recorded in Mark's Gospel. But the appeal is as futile here as in the case of James. It surely could not be much clearer — Jesus speaks explicitly of healing, not dying! He says, 'They will lay their hands on the sick, and they will recover' (Mark 16:18). The defender of any practice is being driven to desperate extremes when the only biblical evidence he can quote is in fact a total denial of the practice.

The *Apostolic Constitution (Sacram unctionem infirmorum)*, issued after the Second Vatican Council, tried to redress the balance by including a petition for healing. The catechism also tries to ease the problem by claiming that the anointing 'is not a sacrament for those only who are at the point of death'. However, it still clings to the old notion of extreme unction when it adds a quotation: 'As soon as anyone of the faithful begins to be in danger of death from sickness or old age, the fitting time for him to receive the sacrament has certainly already arrived' *(Sacrosanctum concilium)*.[8]

There is an additional provision for those who are at the point of death. It is the 'eucharist as viaticum'. The *viaticum* in ordinary Latin usage, as for example in Cicero, meant the provision of money for a journey. So in Rome, with the Latin background, it came to be used as referring to the provision made for the journey through death. The claim is made that this final eucharist 'is the seed of eternal life and the power of resurrection ... the sacrament of passing over from death to life from this world to the Father'.[9]

One might answer these claims by pointing out — as I have already done in reference to many of Rome's theories — that there is a total absence of any biblical evidence for the practice. Furthermore, we need to recall what was said earlier, that the eucharist was never seen as a propitiatory offering to placate the wrath of God. The sacrifice offered once for all needs no renewal, and the great High Priest who offered himself once for all is seated in triumph waiting for his people to join him in glory.

The New Testament does not present death as a journey for which we need provision on the way. Multitudes have died in accidents, or in natural disasters, or with sudden heart attacks. There was no opportunity for such people to have either extreme unction or eucharistic viaticum. But then they never needed either, since Jesus had promised to be with his people whatever the circumstances: 'I give them eternal life, and they shall never perish, and no one shall snatch them out of my hand' (John 10:28).

The Christian does not need to dread death. Paul could write, 'To me to live is Christ, and to die is gain' (Phil. 1:21). As he ended his great exposition of the resurrection of Christ he finished on a note of triumph. In fact he personified death and then mocked the last enemy. Is death the grim reaper to be dreaded? 'No,' cried Paul, and continued triumphantly: 'O death, where is thy victory? O death, where is thy sting?' Final victory is sure: 'Thanks be to God, who gives us the victory through our Lord Jesus Christ' (1 Cor. 15:55,57).

Purgatory

The theory behind penance, that expiation must be offered in addition to accepting the word of pardon, reaches beyond the grave. It points to the notion of purgatory. This theory arose

out of the supposed need to deal with the temporal consequences of sin. Thus the soul who dies in a state of grace does
not necessarily go, as Paul expected, to the presence of the
Lord, but to a time of purging. Medieval preaching and writing
were embellished by an imagination which pictured in horrific
terms the pains of purgatory.

The post-Vatican II world may try to moderate these
excesses, but the idea of a place of purging, where the sins
which were not expiated by penance require further purifying,
still holds. So the catechism insists: 'All who die in God's
grace and friendship, but still imperfectly purified, are indeed
assured of their eternal salvation; but after death they undergo
purification, so as to achieve the holiness necessary to enter the
joy of heaven. The Church gives the name Purgatory to this
final purification of the elect, which is entirely different from
the punishment of the damned.'[10]

The catechism affirms its acceptance of tradition on this
issue, and quotes from the Council of Florence and the Council
of Trent. The former of these two councils maintained concerning those who die in a state of grace 'before having
satisfied by worthy fruits of penance for their sins of commission and omission' that 'Their souls are cleansed after death by
purgatorial penalties.'[11] Trent underlined this and insisted 'that
there is a purgatory and that the souls detained there are helped
by the acts of intercession of the faithful and especially by the
acceptable sacrifice of the altar'.[12]

There is a link between the penance prescribed in the
confessional and the purifying of the soul in purgatory. It is the
theory of indulgences. Allied to the practice of granting
indulgences, and indeed essential to such grants, is the totally
unbiblical notion of the treasury of merit on which the church
draws to provide indulgences either for the living or for the
departed in purgatory. 'An indulgence is a remission before
God of the temporal punishment due to sins whose guilt has

already been forgiven... An indulgence is partial or plenary according as it removes either part or all of the temporal punishment due to sin.'[13]

The 'treasury of merit'

The alleged source of the spiritual largesse which the church dispenses in the form of indulgences is the treasury of merit, a kind of heavenly bank. Its resources which are at the church's disposal consist of the infinite merits of Christ to which are added 'the prayers and good works of the Blessed Virgin Mary, also the prayers and good works of all the saints'.[14] A mathematician commented to me that the idea of adding a finite amount to infinity is meaningless!

The error is, however, far more serious than a mere mathematical absurdity. There is a gross doctrinal fallacy here. It is the notion of works of supererogation. The word is drawn from two Latin words, *'rogo'*, I ask or require, and *'super'*, above. So these good works are assumed to achieve more merit than is required by the person performing them. Hence they may be transferred as surplus merit to the treasury. Jesus himself gave the decisive answer to any such speculation in his words to his disciples: 'So you also, when you have done all that is commanded you, say, "We are unworthy servants; we have only done what was our duty"' (Luke 17:10).

In his parable of the ten virgins he emphasized the point that each one of us is answerable before God. Thus the five virgins could not help the others because they had only enough oil for their own lamps. To try to share out that oil would have left them all in the darkness with none of them able to welcome the bridegroom. Good works in the New Testament can never be superabundant. The standard is beyond our attainment but it still beckons us: 'You, therefore, must be perfect, as your heavenly Father is perfect' (Matt. 5:48). Only one has ever reached that perfection — Jesus the Messiah. Paul speaks for the most godly men and women down the ages when he says, 'Not that I ... am already perfect; but I press on' (Phil. 3:12). Notions of surplus merit and a treasury of merit are alike figments of the ecclesiastical imagination. They are not only absent from Scripture but are incompatible with the rich assurance that we are saved by grace.

Prayers for the dead

Returning to the suggestion that we may pray for the souls in purgatory, we find no grounds in Scripture for the practice of praying for the dead. Rome quotes from the apocryphal book 2 Maccabees. The passage records the deaths in battle of a number of soldiers. Hidden under their tunics were sacred tokens of idols. Judas Maccabeus sent money to Jerusalem to pay for the sacrifice of a sin offering to atone for their idolatry. Then follows the comment which the catechism quotes: 'It is a holy and a wholesome thought to pray for the dead that they may be loosed from their sins' (2 Macc. 12:45).

Apart altogether from the question as to the authority of the apocryphal books, we must surely insist that the action of Judas which they speak of with approval runs completely counter to the catechism. The latter teaches that those who die in mortal sin do not go to heaven, nor even to purgatory, but to hell and are therefore beyond redemption.[15] 'Each man receives his eternal retribution in his immortal soul at the very moment of his death ... either entrance into the blessedness of heaven — through a purification or immediately — or immediate and everlasting damnation.'[16]

Confidence in the face of death

To add to the uncertainty that many feel at the near approach of death, there is the added uncertainty noted earlier where a sacrament is only valid if the priest who administers it has the right intention. The dying man cannot be sure that the priest who hears his confession has the right intention in the sacramental absolution. Nor can he be sure that after death valid eucharists will continue to be offered, or how long the purgation may last. By contrast the gospel speaks quiet assurance. To know that the Good Shepherd is with us in the valley of the shadow of death begets confidence. Assurance comes not by the complexities of a humanly devised sacramental system, but by the solid veracity of Scripture.

We hear God's voice from heaven: '"Blessed are the dead who die in the Lord henceforth." "Blessed indeed," says the Spirit, "that they may rest from their labours"' (Rev. 14:13). With the confidence that the blood of Jesus cleanses completely, so that no purging in an imagined purgatory is required, we can already begin to sing the anthem of heaven: 'To him who loves us and has freed us from our sins by his blood and made us a kingdom, priests to his God and Father, to him be glory and dominion for ever and ever. Amen' (Rev. 1:5-6).

11.
Transubstantiation and the mass

An earlier chapter queried the notion of a priestly and sacramental ministry and it is supremely in the mass that one sees this priestly authority in action. Supernatural power is claimed to be granted to the priest to be an effectual agent in the accomplishment of God's powerful works. Thus it is the priest who is the key figure in the claimed miracle whereby the substance of bread and wine is changed into the body and blood, soul and divinity of Christ. It is the priest who elevates the consecrated bread and calls on the congregation to worship what is declared to be the real presence of the Lord. The word used to describe this miracle is 'transubstantiation'.

By way of preliminary introduction there are three words which require translation or elucidation. The word 'host' comes from the Latin *hostia*, which means 'victim'. The word *'latria'*, which is the worship to be offered, is that which is due to God alone. Earlier, in the chapter on Mary, I noted that Rome has two lesser words, *dulia* and *hyperdulia*, which refer to the veneration of the saints and to the special veneration of Mary. Here, however, the worship of the host is *latria*. It is not surprising therefore — to turn to another key word — that the place where the reserved sacrament is placed is called 'the tabernacle'. This name recalls the Old Testament, in which the place where God manifested his presence prior to the building of the temple was thus designated.

Transubstantiation

To turn to the most significant word, 'transubstantiation', it should be noted at the outset that this theory emerged in the late Middle Ages — the thirteenth century could hardly be called the days of the early church! Even more significant is the fact that the word grew out of medieval philosophy. In their attempt to understand the world in which they lived the philosophers viewed any material object as being composed of two essential qualities — substance and accidents. Thus the alleged miracle in the mass was a total change of the substance of the bread and wine while the accidents remained the same.

When they used the term 'accidents' the word had nothing of the idea of an accident, as used in modern English to describe a mishap of varying severity! Rather it was used to describe the various sensory data available to sight, taste, smell and touch. So a piece of bread has a distinctive flavour; it feels soft; it has a distinctive aroma. These aspects are the 'accidents', while the substance is the essence, the intrinsic character of the bread.

Had the medieval theologians stayed with Scripture they would have continued to hold Augustine's position, where the Lord's Supper is the 'visible word'. Sadly, they tried to compress biblical truth within the confines of transitory philosophical theory. So they claimed that in the miracle of transubstantiation the accidents remained the same but the underlying essence was changed. So the bread might still taste like bread, and if left it might even grow mouldy just like stale bread, but its substance, its essential nature, would have been transformed.

The debate had raged for a long time, but the final settlement was made at the Fourth Lateran Council in 1215. 'The Profession of Faith' declared that in the church, 'The same Jesus Christ is at once priest and victim, whose body and blood are truly contained in the Sacrament of the altar under the species of bread and wine, the bread being transubstantiated into the body by the divine power, and the wine into the blood... And no one can effect this sacrifice but a priest duly ordained.'

The Council of Trent developed the same teaching. Its decree on the eucharist firmly maintained in the chapter on transubstantiation: 'By the consecration of the bread and wine a change is brought about of the whole substance of the bread into the substance of the body of Christ our Lord, and of the whole substance of the wine into the substance of the blood. This change the holy Catholic Church properly and appropriately calls transubstantiation.'[1]

In the previous chapter there were two important additions, in that not only Christ's body and blood but '... his soul and divinity, exist under the form of bread and the blood under the form of wine'. Furthermore the claim is made that 'Christ is whole and entire under the form of bread and under any part of that form; likewise the whole Christ is present under the form of wine and under all its parts.'[2] This surely can only mean that every crumb of the bread, and every drop of the wine becomes, as far as its substance is concerned, Christ himself.

This explains the use of the consecrated host in such services as benediction when the wafer in the monstrance is elevated in blessing the people. It is also claimed as the justification for reserving the host for worship. Trent is emphatic that this worship is *latria* 'which is due to the true God'. The processions on the feast of Corpus Christi are for the same purpose, to evoke worship for the supposed real presence of Christ.

The Council of Trent was so confident on this matter that it was ready to anathematize any who rejected such teaching: 'If anyone shall say that in the holy sacrament of the eucharist Christ, the only begotten Son of God, is not to be adored with the worship of *latria* ... neither to be venerated with a special festive solemnity nor to be solemnly borne about in procession ... or is not to be set publicly before the people to be adored and that the adorers thereof are idolaters — *anathema sit* [Let him be accursed]'.[3]

Critics within Rome may protest that I have been ignoring all the current liturgical changes. This would be a strange protest since Rome's appeal is not only to Scripture but to tradition. I have simply been quoting from these traditions in order that I may be in a position to appeal finally to Scripture. Meanwhile, however, I must ask whether there have been such changes in Rome as to mark a fundamental shift.

The documents of Vatican II introduced new ideas and practices. For example, they allowed, with much caution, the possibility of both the bread and the wine being received by communicants. This was only to be in restricted circumstances decided by the bishops. However, even this limited change was presented in the context of a very firm declaration: 'The dogmatic principles which were laid down by the Council of Trent remaining intact.'[4] So changes such as the encouragement of active participation and the stress on being communicants rather than virtual observers do not alter the basic issue.

Paul VI, who presided over the final days of the council, after the death of John XXIII, made it clear that the many changes which were being introduced must not be allowed to affect the basic dogmatic structures. The conservative reaction was seen in his encyclical *Mysterium Fidei* ('On the holy eucharist'). Progressives might want to use the term 'Lord's Supper' rather than 'the holy sacrifice of the Mass'. They might discuss the issue of the real presence and play with the word 'transignification', which refers to a change of meaning, or significance, rather than a substantial change in the bread and wine. Paul VI, however, would have none of this! He insisted on retaining not only the historic designation 'transubstantiation', but also its essential meaning. He endorsed the veneration of the reserved sacrament and insisted that this veneration meant true worship: 'There has not been a time when she [i.e. the Church] has failed to venerate this great sacrament with the cult of worship which is due to God alone.'[5]

He continued to stress the dogma in his sermon, *'Credo'* — the creed of the people of God: 'We believe that the mysterious presence of the Lord [in the eucharist] is a true, real and substantial presence. Every theological explanation which seeks some understanding of this mystery must, in order to be in accord with the Catholic faith, maintain that the bread and wine have ceased to exist after the consecration so that it is the adorable body and blood of the Lord Jesus.'

Coming up to date we find John Paul II endorsing the continuing tradition. Reflecting on what he sees as the great miracle of transubstantiation, he speaks of the priestly hands which accomplish this mighty change in bread and wine: 'Our greatest commitment consists in exercising this mysterious power over the Body of the Redeemer, and all that is within us should be decisively ordered to this.'[6] It is not surprising therefore that he so wholeheartedly advocates 'various forms of eucharistic devotion: personal prayer before the Blessed Sacrament ... eucharistic benediction, eucharistic processions, eucharistic congresses'.[7]

The Vatican Catechism continues to echo the teaching of Trent and the Fourth Lateran Council: 'In the most blessed sacrament of the Eucharist the body and blood together with the soul and divinity, of our Lord Jesus Christ and therefore the whole Christ is truly, really, and substantially contained.' A word of explanation is added lest anyone might assume that to speak of the real presence in the eucharist is to denigrate as unreal the experience of Christ present in the heart. The presence is real, so it is claimed, in that 'It is presence in the fullest sense, that is to say, it is a substantial presence by which Christ, God and man, makes himself wholly and entirely present.'[8]

It is not surprising therefore that the American bishops were ready to endorse the Roman Catholic charismatic movement since in the latter there was such an endorsement of the real presence. The movement in Ireland had a similar orientation. Thomas Flynn, one of the early leaders, urged a couple of members to assist the work by spending an hour before the blessed sacrament.[9] As we saw in an earlier chapter, a prominent leader in England, Simon Tugwell, quoted approvingly from Thomas Aquinas the comment that 'If there had been a consecrated host reserved at the time of Christ's death, we should have to say that he died also in the reserved host.'[10]

Our starting-point in replying to this central tenet of Roman sacramental teaching is to examine the words of the Saviour when he celebrated the Passover with his disciples. It was the decisive moment when the old covenant ended and the new covenant began. 'This is my body which is for you... This cup is the new covenant in my blood' (1 Cor. 11:24-25). Do these words really undergird the dogma? Is this a statement where the implied change in the bread and wine is simply the starting-point for subsequent dogmatic development?

But surely such harsh literalism makes nonsense of the Lord's words. One thinks of other occasions when he used figurative language to powerful effect. 'I am the door,' he claimed (John 10:7). It would be a nonsensical conclusion to draw to infer that he literally became a door. It would be equally absurd to apply bald literalism to his other claim: 'I am the true vine' (John 15:1). Only a fool would argue that he had changed the substance of the vine to substitute himself. Of course he was using the words figuratively.

To take his words at the Passover meal and to try to force them into a rigid mould is not only to distort what Jesus said, but in fact to open the way for one of the earliest heresies in Christian history. Already within the New Testament we see evidence of the emerging conflict as John insists that we must maintain that 'Jesus Christ has come in the flesh' (1 John 4:2).

Clearly he was facing the kind of teaching, which would later
develop, that rejected the orthodox doctrine of the incarnation.
The early Christians recognized that it was vital to maintain
that the doctrine of the incarnation was not some illusory idea,
but was in fact a solid affirmation of the truth that the Son of
God had truly become one of us. He who was fully God was
also fully man.

That means that at the Last Supper Jesus was present in his
incarnate perfection. It was a human voice which the disciples
heard. The action of setting apart the bread and the wine was
performed by human hands. To accept a literalistic interpretation of the words of institution is to claim that he who reclined
at the table held his body and blood in his own hands. This
surely is not only an affront to common sense but, more
seriously, a denial of the essential integrity of his humanity.

It is significant that the Lord continued to speak of the bread
and wine in terms of their continuing in their natural state and
thus remaining what they were before he spoke. This becomes
clearer when we read the parallel account given by Matthew:
'I tell you I shall not drink again of this fruit of the vine until
that day when I drink it new with you in my Father's kingdom'
(Matt. 26:29; Luke 22:18). Similarly, when Paul records
Jesus' further words they clearly refer to bread and wine in
their natural condition: 'For as often as you eat this bread and
drink the cup, you proclaim the Lord's death until he comes'
(1 Cor. 11:26).

If someone still insists on an unimaginative literalism then
let me reply with an example of literalism in the same context
which shows just how absurd it is to refuse to accept Jesus'
words as figurative. Jesus said, 'This cup is the new covenant
in my blood.' Did he mean that literally, so that the only way
to break the new covenant would be to smash the chalice? Was
the cup subject to a substantial change? 'That is nonsense',
someone objects, and I heartily concur, but insist that it is
equally ridiculous to claim that Jesus' words concerning the

bread are subject to the same kind of rigid explanation as would produce nonsense if it was applied to the cup!

One must also take into account the fact that Jesus had not yet died when he spoke these words. His body had not yet been given in that final act of obedience when he went to the cross. His blood was still in his veins and had not been shed at Calvary. So it is surely impossible to maintain that when he spoke of his blood 'poured out for many' this had already taken place. Jesus, knowing as he did the eternal purposes of God and the prophetic Scriptures of the Old Testament, could speak with certainty as if what was still in the future was already a reality. For him the sacrifice was in the immediate future. For us it is in the past. But because it was still to happen as far as he was concerned it is surely wrong to claim that the wine *had already* been changed so that the blood *not yet shed* was already in the consecrated cup.

A very helpful comment on this matter comes from the great theologian of the fifth century, Augustine of Hippo in North Africa. He gives practical guidance for determining whether a passage is to be taken literally or figuratively: 'If a passage is preceptive, and either forbids a crime or wickedness or enjoins usefulness or charity, it is not figurative. But if it seems to command a crime or wickedness, or to forbid usefulness or kindness, it is figurative. "Unless you eat", he says, "the flesh of the Son of Man, and drink his blood, you have no life in you." He appears to enjoin wickedness, or a crime. It is a figure, therefore, teaching us that we partake of the benefits of the Lord's passion, and that we must sweetly and profitably treasure up in our memories that his flesh was crucified and wounded for us.'[11]

There may be a further objection raised as we endeavour to understand the solemn warning of the apostle: 'Whoever, therefore, eats the bread or drinks the cup of the Lord in an unworthy manner will be guilty of profaning the body and blood of the Lord' (1 Cor. 11:27). If the unworthy communicants do not receive the actual body and blood of the Lord — as Rome claims they do — why should their receiving the bread and wine be such a serious issue? The answer, as so often in Bible study, is to be found in the context. Why did Paul introduce the discussion about the Lord's Supper? It was because there had been such a selfish display of thoughtlessness by the richer members of the fellowship. They seem to have had a supper together as well as celebrating the communion. But whereas this should have provided an opportunity for thoughtful and considerate behaviour shown in loving concern for the poorer members, what actually happened was something very different and Paul rebukes them: 'For in eating, each one goes ahead with his own meal, and one is hungry and another is drunk' (1 Cor. 11:21). Paul is indignant. They could have eaten and drunk at home. Why had they to meet in an ostensible show of fellowship only to humiliate fellow Christians?

It was in this situation that Paul pointed them to the Lord's behaviour on the night when he was betrayed. He had declared to his disciples that he was among them as their servant, hence his humble adoption of the slave's rôle as he knelt to wash their feet. Then he gave them an abiding ordinance. It was essentially a fellowship meal. The very term 'communion' speaks of sharing together.

So the bread was broken for sharing around and the cup was for all to share: 'Do this, as often as you drink it, in remembrance of me.' Matthew in his version emphasizes the sharing aspect: 'Drink of it, all of you.' Since the Lord's Supper was to be the visible word declaring God's gospel it was sheer profanity to share in such a fellowship meal while at the same time breaching that fellowship by personal greed or inconsiderate behaviour.

What then are we to say about Paul's further warning about not 'discerning the [Lord's] body'? Paul himself gave the answer at an earlier stage. He reminded these Corinthian believers that in spite of their past history of immorality and

iniquity they were now the people of God. 'Do you not know
that you are God's temple and that God's Spirit dwells in you?'
(1 Cor. 3:16). So the living members of the church are the
dwelling-place of the Lord. That is why the factions he had
been describing earlier in that same chapter are now seen as
destroying God's temple.

Paul dealt with this matter again, once again in the context
of divisive behaviour, when he handled the issue of spiritual
gifts. For any to become proud because they had been granted
gifts was to fail to see that the reason why the gifts were
bestowed was 'for the common good' (1 Cor. 12:7). It was
with this emphasis on mutual service that he declares their
true status: 'Now you are the body of Christ and individually
members of it' (1 Cor. 12:27). The aim is that 'there may be
no discord in the body' (1 Cor. 12:25), but that love should
reign.

In each of these three situations there was evidence of pride,
selfishness and subsequent division. The real problem, of
which these things were the symptoms, was that they had
failed to discern the Lord's body. These poorer members and
those who were apparently less gifted were all members of the
body and must always be seen in that light. One of the reasons
for the institution of the Lord's Supper was that this unity
should be declared in the loving fellowship gathered at the
Lord's table.

There is a further important truth which is highlighted in the
Lord's Supper and is obscured by the theory of transubstantiation. It is the hope of Christ's return at the end of the age.
Before his death Jesus prepared his disciples for his bodily
removal from them, and then encouraged them by using this
as the basis for the promised coming of the Holy Spirit. Thus
the history of the church dawns in the two events, the ascension of Jesus and the pouring out of the Spirit at Pentecost.
They would, he had said, 'see [him] no more' (John 16:16), but

they would not be left like orphans, for in the person of the Holy Spirit he would come to them.

So the Lord's Supper would be celebrated 'until he comes' (1 Cor. 11:26). How then are we to interpret that coming? The answer was given by the angels to the wondering disciples as they stood gazing into heaven while the Lord ascended and they saw him no more: 'This Jesus, who was taken up from you into heaven, will come in the same way as you saw him go into heaven' (Acts 1:11). How had they seen him go? It was in bodily fashion. Again and again they had met him after his resurrection. He had assured them that they were not seeing ghosts or suffering from some delusion. So he commanded them: 'See my hands and my feet, that it is I myself; handle me, and see; for a spirit has not flesh and bones as you see that I have' (Luke 24:39). He even went so far as to eat some fish to demonstrate that his body was real. Hence the angel's promise pointed to a bodily return.

The Lord has, however, ascended. He is now in the glory of his Father's presence and his bodily presence on earth will only be realized on the day of his return. This does not leave his church as the fellowship of the absent Lord. His Spirit makes the presence of Jesus an experienced reality. Yet written across every communion service is the great reminder that this is only 'until he comes'. We dare not presume to be wiser than God and require a bodily presence *now*, when he has insisted on it being *then*. Now we rejoice that he is here in and through the Holy Spirit.

Another distortion of biblical truth emerges from the theory of transubstantiation. It is the withholding of the cup from the congregation. If the theory were true then one can understand the hesitation over the wine. In the case of the wafer it can be put directly into the mouth with little likelihood of dropping it. There would clearly be greater risk of spilling the wine as the cup is passed from one to another. If substantially it had become the blood of Christ, then such a spillage would be very serious. The safer procedure would be to withhold the cup, but this represents a grievous interference with the Lord's clearly declared intention when he instituted the supper.

It is in fact a wilful rejection of the plain words of the Lord. Surely he could not have spoken more clearly than when he said, 'Drink of it, all of you' (Matt. 26:27). Lest anyone should try to evade this by claiming that only the apostles were present at the Last Supper, the answer to such a suggestion is found in Paul's words to the congregation in Corinth: 'As often as you eat this bread and drink the cup, you proclaim the Lord's death' (1 Cor. 11:26). Clearly participation in the Lord's Supper entailed both eating and drinking.

To omit what the Lord commanded is to reject his authority. To maintain that it is sufficient to receive only the bread and to justify this by claiming that in substance it has become the body and blood, soul and divinity of Christ, as Trent declared, is to add insult to injury. It is to use a medieval theory to justify plain disobedience to the word of the Lord himself.

If we were to make appeal to tradition, as Rome delights to do, we could well cite in this connection the homily of John Chrysostom: 'Whereas under the old covenant the priests ate some things and the laymen others; and it was not lawful for the people to partake of those things of which the priest partook; it is not so now, but one body is placed before all and one cup.'[12]

I recall some years ago giving a lecture to a majority Roman Catholic audience in Waterford. A friendly old priest raised the issue that, in his view, I had no doctrine of the real presence. My reply was that we often began a service of worship with the hymn, 'Jesus, stand among us in thy risen power.' At the Lord's Supper we might well sing together a hymn composed by one of our great preachers, Charles Spurgeon:

Amidst us our Beloved stands
And bids us view his pierced hands,
Points to his wounded feet and side,
Blest emblems of the Crucified.

My conclusion was that we did believe in the real presence but it is located not in the elements of bread and wine, but in the hearts of his believing people. In rejecting transubstantiation we do not advocate an absent Christ. Rather we affirm a spiritual presence, as the Holy Spirit, proceeding from the Father and the Son, constitutes the congregation as the temple of the Spirit and the body of Christ.

The mass

The mass as a holy sacrifice has already been in view in our consideration of the nature of priesthood, where the epistle to the Hebrews was invoked to emphasize the unique priesthood of Christ. On the one hand, this was foreshadowed by the Levitical priesthood and, on the other, by fulfilling the Old Testament priestly image, at the same time it abrogated that priesthood. Thus Jesus is the only mediator and believers need no other priest but him.

This inevitably led to a consideration of the issue of sacrifice, since Jesus was not only the great High Priest but the Lamb of God. He was both priest and victim. The key to understanding the significance of his priestly offering is the constantly repeated emphasis of Hebrews, and of so many of the other epistles, that the offering was once for all, and never to be repeated. This brings us back to the claim that the eucharist is a continuing sacrifice. It was necessary to interpose the examination of the theory of transubstantiation as the claim that there is a miraculous change in the substance of the bread and wine is obviously of crucial significance as we resume the study of 'the holy sacrifice of the mass'.

It is easy in debating a controversial issue to misrepresent what the other side actually believes. It is not surprising therefore that Roman Catholics are indignant when a critic speaks of them repeating what happened at Calvary and thus multiplying the offering. They maintain vigorously that the mass is not a separate or independent sacrifice, but is the same sacrifice now made present because of the mysterious presence of Christ in the consecrated host.

The best answer to misrepresentation is to go back to the actual statements of Roman councils and papal declarations. We go back to the Council of Trent and note that the great Counter-Reformation council is still being quoted in the catechism. So it is not simply an interesting statement from the sixteenth century. It is part of that ongoing tradition that Rome so reveres and that has been put on a level with Scripture as a fount of revelation.

The theologians at Trent were certainly explicit in declaring how they saw the nature of the sacrifice on the altar: 'At the Last Supper on the night when he was betrayed in order to leave his beloved spouse the church a visible sacrifice (as the nature of man demands) by which the bloody sacrifice which he was once for all to accomplish on the cross would be represented, its memory perpetuated until the end of the world and its salutary power applied for the forgiveness of sins... He offered his body and blood under the species of bread and wine to God the Father.'[13]

Before we continue to examine other statements made at Trent, two points need to be made immediately. It is strange theology to claim that what 'the nature of man demands' is a valid reason for formulating a dogma. To satisfy that demand by a theory of continuing sacrifice is to make the misguided thinking of men, rather than the Word of God, the arbiter of truth.

Also in claiming that at the Last Supper the Lord offered his body and blood, Trent went right against Scripture by anticipating the sacrifice of Calvary and locating the self-sacrifice of Jesus at the supper. Yet Jesus himself contradicted such a notion. As they reclined at the table Jesus clearly distinguished between the supper and the cross — witness his words: 'I have earnestly desired to eat this passover with you *before I suffer*' (Luke 22:15, italics added). So the sacrificial suffering was emphatically not at the table but on the cross!

Trent goes on to claim that 'In this divine sacrifice which is celebrated in the mass, the same Christ who offered himself in a bloody manner on the altar of the cross is contained and is offered in an unbloody manner. Therefore the holy council teaches that this sacrifice is truly propitiatory.'[14] All this is backed up with one of the many curses pronounced by Trent: 'If anyone shall say that the sacrifice of the mass is only one of praise and thanksgiving or that it is ... not a propitiatory one; or that it profits only him who receives communion and ought not to be offered for the living and the dead, for sins, punishments, satisfactions and other necessities — *anathema sit* [let him be accursed].'[15]

So we are surely not misrepresenting Trent when we conclude it presents the mass as a sacrifice which procures God's pardon and favour; also that it is a powerful reinforcement of our prayers. To use two technical terms it is propitiatory and impetratory. A propitiation is a sacrifice offered whereby God's anger is assuaged and he becomes favourable — he becomes propitious! The more unusual word, 'impetratory', comes from a Latin word *impetrare*, meaning 'to bring to pass'. So the sacrifice of the mass may be directed to certain goals which the offerer hopes to reach, or benefits which he hopes to receive.

The popes have continued to make the same point. Pius XII wrote, 'It must be emphasized again and again that the eucharistic sacrifice is essentially the unbloody immolation of the divine Victim, an immolation mystically manifested in the separation of the sacred species (i.e. bread and wine) and the offering made of them to the Eternal Father.'[16] The word 'immolation' is derived from the Latin *immolare*, to offer a sacrifice.

The Second Vatican Council continued the theme in the decree on the priestly ministry and life: 'It is for the priests to teach the faithful to offer the divine Victim in the sacrifice of the mass to God the Father.'[17] Paul VI, who presided over the closing stages of the council, reinforced the ideas of eucharistic sacrifice in the encyclical on the holy eucharist to which I referred earlier. There I pointed to his wholehearted endorsement of transubstantiation, and his encouragement of the worship of the sacramental presence. It should also be noted that he made no concession on the offering of Christ on the altar: 'The church has always offered it [the sacrifice] not only for the sins, punishment satisfactions and needs of the faithful still alive but also for those who have died in Christ but are not yet fully cleansed.'[18]

John Paul II went even further as he spoke of the priest offering the sacrifice. He gave the sacrificing priest a very high status and, as we saw in the chapter 'Why Priests?', a grossly unbiblical one. Thus in an encyclical he wrote, 'The priest offers the holy sacrifice *in persona Christi*; this means more than offering in the name of or in the place of Christ. *In persona* means in specific sacramental identification with the eternal High Priest.'[19]

Here we are at the heart of the matter and here we discover how remote the papal and conciliar teaching is from the Scripture. Here, by plain implication, is a denial of the perfection of Christ's offering. We are back to the rebuttal of these eucharistic theories by the letter to the Hebrews and by Paul's recurring emphasis on the finished work of Christ. The sacrifice on the cross was totally complete. The cry of victory, 'It is finished!' was echoed from heaven by the resurrection from the dead. The advocacy on behalf of his people in heaven is not a continuing self-sacrifice to procure a propitiation. That has already been procured. Jesus fully obeyed his Father's will. He took the burden of his people's sins upon him. He has been welcomed back to the Father's presence and the finality of his sacrifice has been declared in the hymn of praise: 'To him who loves us and has freed us from our sins by his blood' (Rev. 1:5). His love continues and is therefore spoken of in the present tense, but his atoning work, having been perfected, is spoken of as a past event and needs no supplementary offering.

When God brought all things into being in the work of creation he reached the point where he saw that work complete. God saw that it was very good! Then comes a vivid comment on the finality of that work: 'God ... rested from all his work which he had done' (Gen. 2:2). He did not lapse into inactivity, but now his work would be to sustain the creation. He would not be continuing creation, for that was complete.

Similarly, when Christ Jesus accomplished the new creation it was by a like demonstration of sovereign and gracious power. There is also a vivid indication that the work was done: 'He sat down' (Heb. 1:3). He would not lapse into inaction. He would continue his work of intercession at the right hand of the Father. But he would not need to add further offerings to the already accepted ransom price which he had fully paid. Now, just as the triune God rested and yet sustained the work of creation, so Christ has sat down on the throne and yet still ministers to his people through his Holy Spirit, the true Vicar of Christ.

What popes and councils have failed to see is the true significance of the Lord's Supper. They talk and write as if the Supper was a means of reminding God about Calvary, when in fact it is not God but we who need that reminder. The apostle Paul brings that truth home to us when he declares: 'For as often as you eat this bread and drink the cup, you proclaim the Lord's death until he comes.' Ronald Knox translated with equal felicity: 'So it is the Lord's death which you are heralding.' The Greek word *kataggello* which is used here is employed thirteen times in the Acts of the Apostles and the letters of Paul, to describe the preaching of the gospel where the preacher is a proclaimer or a herald. Such preaching is obviously directly to men and women. We pray to God and offer praise to God, but we preach to men. So when Paul speaks here of proclaiming the Lord's death he is not suggesting a spreading of the sacrifice of Christ before God, in much the same way that the Levitical priests waved the offering. This is not an elevation of the host God-wards. Rather it is a declaration of the gospel to the worshipper. We are back to the basic interpretation of the sacraments as the *verba visibilia,* the visible words, by which the word preached audibly by the lips of the proclaimer is visually preached so that the visible word reinforces the audible word.

It must also be noted that this proclamation is the outcome of eating and drinking. It is not the result of some liturgical action like the ringing of a bell or the elevation of the wafer. It is rather the acts of eating and drinking which emphasize not only the gracious gift of our God, but also our glad appropriation of the blessings God delights to bestow.

The comunion is also a fellowship meal. Paul did not single out one person who did the proclaiming. In the preaching ministry clearly one man commissioned by the Holy Spirit declares God's message. But in the Lord's Supper Paul saw them all sharing in the proclamation. As the bread is shared and the cup passed from hand to hand each communicant is a herald to his or her fellows: 'Hallelujah — our glorious Saviour has paid once and for all the price of our redemption.' Let us keep the feast and proclaim to one another his gospel.

12.
Justified

'Justified by grace alone through faith alone in Christ alone' — this was the basic theme of what came to be called the Protestant Reformation. It was not simply a compressed doctrinal statement produced by a gathering of theologians, though it has stimulated theological debate ever since. It was, rather, the grateful response hammered out on the anvil of one man's soul. Martin Luther had struggled with the most fundamental of all questions: 'How may I, a sinner, stand before a holy God and be accepted?' The flame of faith kindled by the Spirit in one man's conscience was to burn strongly in the lives of many.

Yet, it must be remembered, Luther appeared quite late in Christian history, sixteen centuries after the incarnation of the Son of God and the conversion of the apostle Paul. So justification by faith is not some theory dreamed up by a German monk. The apostle Paul had struggled with the same problem and had not only found the answer in Christ his Saviour, but had been led by the Spirit to pen what has rightly been seen as the classic writing on the doctrine of justification by faith — the epistle of Paul to the Romans. It was in reading that book that Augustine, that great thinker of the early centuries, found peace with God. It was in studying that same epistle that Luther, an Augustinian monk, also came to a joyful assurance of acceptance where formerly there had only been questioning and gloom.

It is not immediately apparent to an English-speaking reader who turns to the letter to the Romans that the terms 'justification' and 'righteousness' belong to the same family group of words. This is brought out clearly in the Greek language, which was for Paul, and for most folk around the Mediterranean, the common tongue. So righteousness *(dikaiosune)* justification *(dikaiosis)* and to justify *(dikaioun)* belong to each other. Righteousness is what God requires from those whom he has created. Justification is the means by which that righteousness is realized in the life of a sinner. To justify is to declare the acquittal of the guilty sinner and his acceptance by his Creator.

The word 'righteousness' has, as its core element, the basic word 'right'. If we recall our early schooldays we will doubtless remember arithmetic homework being marked either right or wrong, where the distinction was between correct and incorrect. Later we may have been asked a question in a history lesson where the query was introduced by the phrase 'True or false?' School also recalls the moral emphasis that we must distinguish in our conduct between right and wrong. Thus the word 'right' embraces the spectrum of meanings — correct, true, measuring up to a standard, morally acceptable. So righteousness means reaching a standard, speaking or acting in truth, conforming to a moral demand.

In the Bible, God alone is in an absolute sense righteous. This does not mean that he measures up to a standard of truth and goodness, since he himself is the standard. It means rather that God speaks and acts consistently with his own divine nature. To lie or deceive would be to act inconsistently with his character as the God of truth. To act wrongly would be a violation of his own holiness. To exhibit flaws in speech or action would be to deny his utter perfection. Abraham summed it up so well: 'Shall not the Judge of all the earth do right?' (Gen. 18:25). Such a righteous God will obviously require righteousness from those who worship him.

Since God is righteous in his deeds it follows that when he takes the great step of becoming incarnate the result will be a human life of similarly perfect righteousness. Hence the apostle John speaks of the Saviour as 'Jesus Christ the righteous' (1 John 2:1). A man who saw him from a very different perspective, the centurion in charge of the crucifixion, paid a like tribute: 'Certainly this man was innocent!' (Luke 23:47). Pilate's wife warned her husband: 'Have nothing to do with that righteous man' (Matt. 27:19). Yet beyond the tributes of his friends and the grudging concession of his enemies, there was the supreme testimony from heaven: 'Thou art my beloved Son; with thee I am well pleased' (Luke 3:22).

When therefore this God demands righteousness from us it is against the background of God's revelation of the standard by which the righteousness required of us is to be assessed. God has revealed this standard in the stringent requirements of the law of Moses. He has written those requirements on the hearts of all men (Rom. 2:15). Above all, he has displayed that standard in the perfection of one human life, that of Jesus, who demonstrated what righteousness means both in life and at the point of death. In John's words, 'The Word became flesh and dwelt among us, full of grace and truth' (John 1:14).

The human response to God's requirements is summed up by the apostle Paul in the first three chapters of the epistle to the Romans. In the world at large there is not only an absence of such righteousness, but its total rejection. This, as Paul argued, follows inevitably from man's rejection of God. So Paul wrote of the wrath of God being 'revealed ... against all ungodliness and wickedness of men who by their wickedness suppress the truth' (Rom. 1:18). The word 'wickedness' could literally be translated 'unrighteousness'. What makes their sin even worse is that they go further down the road of moral perversion, not only delighting in unrighteousness, but approving those who engage in such practices.

Nor did Paul allow the religious person to escape the indictment. He wrote with deep feeling since he himself had come along this very route. A facile condemnation of the blatantly ungodly had led him to a conviction that religious zeal and a conformity to God's law were the path to righteousness, and so to acceptance. But Paul had left that attitude behind him. Outward observance is one thing; the state of the heart is another. The religious man ends up in self-righteousness, which is as much an abomination in God's sight as open ungodliness. So Paul reached the climax of his indictment with the assertion: 'None is righteous, no, not one' (Rom. 3:10). For us to submit to this verdict on our state is to realize how vital the question is: 'How may I, a sinner, stand before this holy God and be accepted?' Paul's answer is Christ, who is our righteousness.

Justified

This brings us back to the word 'justify'. How can God, who is morally perfect, pardon a convicted sinner? Surely there must be some change in the sinner's character if sin is not to be condoned. Paul argued in his second letter to the church in Corinth (2 Cor. 5:21) that God's declaration of acceptance is fully consistent with God's justice because of what Christ has done for us. He is continuing to use the word 'justify' in its literal sense, just as it was used in his day in the lawcourts, for, let it be noted carefully, the word was essentially a legal term meaning 'to acquit', to declare 'not guilty'.

At this point the Council of Trent disagreed. It asserted that 'to justify' did not mean to reckon the sinner to be righteous.

Rather it meant to make the sinner holy, so that he would be in a position to attempt to measure up to God's requirements. 'Justification ... is not only the remission of sins but the sanctification and renewal of the interior man through the voluntary reception of grace.'[1] The Vatican Catechism endorses the teaching of Trent and claims that for God 'to justify us' means 'to cleanse us from our sins and to communicate to us the righteousness of God through faith in Jesus Christ and through Baptism'.[2]

Hans Küng wrote his significant work on justification while still having the authorization of the Vatican as a recognized theologian. The loss of that authorization came later, after his trenchant critique of papal infallibility. It was therefore as a Catholic teacher that he wrote what was really a reinterpretation of the findings of Trent, if not a reversal! He insisted that 'Sacred Scripture has an absolute precedence which no other theological argument can whittle away.'[3]

It is not surprising therefore to find him affirming that 'Justification is the declaration of justice by God in a court judgment... Justification is the declaration of justice by the merciful God.'[4] That leads him to maintain that Paul never speaks of self-justification by man. '*Dikaioun* (to justify) is used either in speaking of God who himself justifies (Rom. 3:26,30; 4:5; 8:30,33; Gal. 3:8) or of man who does not justify but is justified (Rom. 2:13; 3:20,24-28; 4:2; 5:1,9; 1 Cor. 4:4; 6:11; Gal. 2:16ff; 3:11.24; 5:4; Titus 3:7).'[5]

The issue was made abundantly clear by Paul in the verse to which I have already referred briefly. It is one of the most arresting statements in the New Testament as to the radical nature of the atoning death of Christ. 'For our sake he [God] made him [Christ] to be sin who knew no sin, so that in him we might become the righteousness of God' (2 Cor. 5:21). Clearly the statement that God made Christ sin could in no sense mean that God imparted to his Son sinfulness of character. After all, the cross was the climax of his life of righteousness in that he carried his obedience to his Father's will to the ultimate point: 'He ... became obedient unto death, even death on a cross' (Phil. 2:8).

If then we rule out the false notion that God made Christ an actual sinner we are left with the inevitable conclusion that, since Christ was the representative of his people whom he had come to save, God set their sin to his account. He was reckoned to be a sinner though he was without sin, because their sin was imputed to him. It was a judicial act by the divine Judge. Hence the penalty of death had to follow, since 'The wages of sin is death' (Rom. 6:23).

Paul's statement in 2 Corinthians 5:21 is a balanced parallel where what happened to Christ is set over against what happens to believers. If then one side of the comparison is to be interpreted in harmony with the other, we are forced to conclude that what happened to believers is also a judicial act. If Christ was not made an actual sinner, no more are we made actually righteous. Rather, just as God set our sinfulness to his account, so he has set Christ's righteousness to ours. Our acceptance by God is not due to the evidence of an inner change in us. If it depended on this we should always have a very dubious hope of such acceptance. But because the righteousness of Christ is utterly perfect, when God reckons that righteousness to our account we may rejoice in our acceptance, our justification.

By grace

We come to the next key word: we are justified by *grace* alone. God's grace is his free and undeserved favour to sinners. The initiative is with God, who formed the plan of salvation. Paul put it thus: 'He [God] chose us in him [Christ] before the foundation of the world' (Eph. 1:4). In the fulness of time he sent his Son. In his own appointed time he graciously works in the sinner eliciting faith in Christ. But grace excludes all other contributory factors. There is no place for human merit. There is no room for human righteousness, since in the prophetic words of Isaiah, 'All our righteous deeds are like a polluted garment' (Isa. 64:6).

There is a frequent insistence in Scripture on God's initiative. God always takes the first step in drawing the sinner to himself. Thus Jesus, while giving his gracious invitation to sinners to come to him, balanced this with the reminder that behind our coming to him is God's coming to us: 'All that the Father gives me will come to me; and him who comes to me I will not cast out' (John 6:37). Lest there should still be any lingering self-confidence, he added further emphasis: 'No one can come to me unless the Father who sent me draws him' (John 6:44). He stressed the point later when he again emphasized his divine initiative: 'You did not choose me, but I chose you' (John 15:16).

The apostolic testimony echoed this focus on the free grace of the sovereign God. The sinner is seen as spiritually blind, but 'The God who said, "Let light shine out of darkness," … has shone in our hearts to give the light of the knowledge of the glory of God in the face of Christ' (2 Cor. 4:6). The sinner is not only spiritually blind but incapable by natural reason alone to understand the simplicity of the gospel unless God enlightens his mind. The man who does not have the Holy Spirit 'does not receive the gifts of the Spirit of God, for they are folly to him, and he is not able to understand them because they are spiritually discerned' (1 Cor. 2:14). The climax of this total rejection of human ability comes in Paul's use of the analogy of death and resurrection. The sinner is by nature 'dead through the trespasses and sins in which you once walked' (Eph. 2:1-2). Clearly a dead man is incapable of any response.

The outlook seems hopeless but then Paul bursts in with his triumphant: 'But God, who is rich in mercy, out of the great love with which he loved us, even when we were dead through our trespasses, made us alive together with Christ (by grace you have been saved)' (Eph. 2:4-5).

Paul's conclusion sounds the death-knell of any appeal to human merit: 'By grace you have been saved through faith; and this is not your own doing, it is the gift of God — not because of works, lest any man should boast' (Eph. 2:8). So even in the exercise of faith we are utterly indebted to God's grace.

Someone may object that this reduces man to a kind of spiritual robot and makes the preaching of the gospel superfluous. By way of answer one might refer to the raising of Lazarus recorded by John. When Jesus stood outside the tomb where the corpse was beginning to putrefy it must have seemed to some the height of absurdity for him to call out, 'Lazarus, come out' (John 11:43). Indeed it must have seemed utterly insensitive in view of the expected anticlimax of a failure which would shatter the sisters' raised hopes. Instead it was a powerful demonstration that the word of Christ is a living, and indeed a life-giving, word. So the apparent absurdity of preaching the gospel to a sinner 'dead through trespasses and sins' is nothing of the sort. The gospel not only summons to faith, but elicits the faith which it commands.

To use a human analogy, a very happily married woman may recall with some amusement her husband's initial vigorous overtures and she may comment, 'He swept me off my feet.' Obviously she is not referring to a violent assault to which she was forced to respond! Rather, it is a vivid way of saying that such was the initiative of his love that she gladly, freely and willingly responded. So the faith which responds to grace is no conditioned reflex, but the glad response of one whose enlightened mind has glimpsed something of the love of God and the condescending mercy of the Saviour.

Through faith

Faith is not the mere acceptance of a set of religious truths presented by the church. Nor is it the establishment of a relationship between an individual and a church fellowship. It is not simply orthodoxy or church membership, important though these are. It is rather a personal trust in a welcoming Saviour. Prompted by the grace of God, faith is elicited by the Word. Thus Paul explains its emergence: 'So faith comes from what is heard, and what is heard comes by the preaching of Christ' (Rom. 10:17). As the word of the gospel is declared the hearer not only grasps what formerly was beyond his ken, but feels an inner compulsion which is due, not to some kind of psychological manipulation by a preacher, but to the loving tenderness of the God who offers mercy 'without money and without price' (Isa. 55:1).

Roman Catholicism, however, has a different message and one which robs the Christian of the kind of assurance which John saw as the birthright of the believer when he wrote his first epistle: 'I write this to you who believe in the name of the Son of God, that you may know that you have eternal life' (1 John 5:13). Instead we meet the conclusion of the Council of Trent: 'If one considers his own weakness and his defective disposition, he may well be fearful and anxious as to his state of grace, as nobody knows with the certainty of faith, which permits of no error, that he has achieved the grace of God.'[6]

Lying behind the uncertainty is the claim of Trent that the grace by which we are justified may be lost, and actually is lost by every grievous sin.[7] This teaching is repeated by the Vatican Catechism in its teaching on penance, which is described as 'the second plank [of salvation] after the shipwreck which is the loss of grace'.[8] The reason for such a loss of grace is noted earlier in the same paragraph, which speaks of those 'who, since Baptism, have fallen into grave sin and have thus lost their baptismal grace'. So justification may be lost and

regained and lost again! It becomes a fluctuating inner righteousness which may come and go.

Certainly this is far removed from the unassailable verdict
of God when he justifies the sinner. It is because of his
unshakeable confidence in his justification that Paul can
mount a powerful challenge: 'Who shall bring any charge
against God's elect? It is God who justifies' (Rom. 8:33). The
background of this assurance is not a bout of wishful thinking.
It is rather an understanding of the unbroken and unbreakable
chain of divine purposes, each link of which is seen to be
guaranteed: 'For those whom he foreknew he also predestined
... and those whom he predestined he also called; and those
whom he called he also justified; and those whom he justified
he also glorified' (Rom. 8:29-30).

Paul, like the other apostolic writers, returned again and
again to the same theme. He assured the Philippian believers:
'And I am sure that he who began a good work in you will bring
it to completion at the day of Jesus Christ' (Phil. 1:6). He
shared this same assurance with Timothy: 'I know whom I
have believed, and I am sure that he is able to guard until that
Day what has been entrusted to me' — a note gives an
alternative translation: 'what I have entrusted to him' (2 Tim.
1:12).

This assurance is so confident because it is rooted firmly in
the promises of God. When Jesus spoke of himself as the Good
Shepherd he added his pledge: 'I give them eternal life and
they shall never perish, and no one shall snatch them out of my
hand' (John 10:28). Jesus reinforced this pledge by emphasizing his role within the Trinity: 'My Father, who has given them
to me, is greater than all, and no one is able to snatch them out
of the Father's hand. I and the Father are one' (John 10:29).

Yet another ground for confidence is the reality of Jesus'
ministry of intercession for each one of his believing disciples.
That life of prayer was seen in what is often referred to as his

high priestly prayer, recorded by the apostle John: 'I am praying for them; I am not praying for the world but for those whom thou hast given me, for they are thine' (John 17:9). That ministry on earth in the days of his incarnation continues in heaven. Because his unique priesthood is permanent, 'He is able for all time to save those who draw near to God through him, since he always lives to make intercession for them' (Heb. 7:25).

A further objection emerges to challenge this insistence on faith alone. What about good works — are they not an important, and indeed an essential, accompaniment of faith? Did James not say in his epistle that Abraham was justified by works, leading to the conclusion: 'You see that a man is justified by works and not by faith alone'? (James 2:23-24). The alleged difference between Paul and James seems at first sight to give credence to the vigorous repudiation by the Council of Trent of the claim that justification is by faith alone.

So the anathemas are pronounced: 'If anyone says that the sinner is justified by faith alone in the sense that nothing else is required by way of co-operation in order to obtain the grace of justification, anathema sit.'[9] 'If anyone says that justifying faith is nothing else than confidence in the divine mercy that remits sins on account of Christ, or that it is this confidence alone that justifies us *anathema sit.*'[10]

Closer study of what Paul and James are actually saying should, however, lead to the conclusion that they are basically in agreement. James is clearly concerned to challenge those who had made a profession of faith but gave little or no sign that their profession was anything more than mere words. True faith leads to fruitful living. Thus James rebukes the person who 'thinks he is religious, and does not bridle his tongue' (James 1:26). The verdict is clear: the man is deceiving himself. By contrast a true faith leads to benevolence towards the needy and a rejection of the standard of the world.

Paul makes the same point. Having insisted that our justification is 'not because of works', he immediately qualifies
what he has just said and emphasizes that we are 'created in
Christ Jesus for good works, which God prepared beforehand,
that we should walk in them' (Eph. 2:9-10). So faith is *without*
works but also *with a view to* good works. It has been well said
that faith alone never remains alone. The contrast is surely
between the root of the tree and the fruit. Good works are the
fruit which demonstrate that the tree is alive; they themselves
do not produce the life, but are produced by it.

Paul demonstrated this also in the letter to the Romans. He
envisages the objector who misuses the truth of justification to
argue: 'What shall we say then? Are we to continue in sin that
grace may abound?' Paul's reaction to this perverted attempt
to justify self-indulgence is passionate: 'By no means! How
can we who died to sin still live in it?' (Rom. 6:1-2). Behind
the testimony of both James and Paul we hear the same
message from Jesus: 'Not everyone who says to me, "Lord,
Lord" shall enter the kingdom of heaven, but he who does the
will of my Father who is in heaven' (Matt. 7:21).

Original sin

The failure of Trent and subsequent teachers to accept the total
rejection of good works prior to justification has its roots in a
more fundamental error. When God in the act of creation
reached the climax he created man: 'Let us make man in our
image, after our likeness' (Gen. 1:26). He created one who was
righteous, in that he was pleasing in God's sight, with his
physical, mental and spiritual faculties all in perfect harmony.
It was in the integrity of Adam's human nature that the life of
God himself was reflected. Thus the phrase has been coined to

speak of his original righteousness — that is, the righteousness of the man who was the origin of the human race. The conclusion is that God saw that everything was 'very good' (Gen. 1:31).

By contrast Rome has seen original righteousness as an additional gift *(donum superadditum)*. As a consequence there are opposing conclusions as to the nature of the Fall when, as Paul wrote, 'Sin came into the world through one man' (Rom. 5:12). Adam's trespass has been appropriately described as original sin since in Adam we meet its origin. There would be agreement between evangelicals and Catholics on the origin of sin but there is a wide gulf of disagreement over its consequences. If Rome is right in its claim that original righteousness was an added gift, then the Fall meant the forfeiting of the gift without doing more than injuring man's moral, mental and spiritual integrity.

This is in fact what Rome claims. Man is deprived, not depraved; he is wounded spiritually, but not killed, though in fact God had warned, 'You shall die' (Gen. 2:17). So the catechism affirms concerning original sin: 'It is a deprivation of original holiness and justice [i.e. righteousness], but human nature has not been totally corrupted: it is wounded in the natural powers proper to it, subject to ignorance, suffering and the dominion of death.'[11]

This all falls far short of the indictment in Genesis: 'The Lord saw that the wickedness of man was great in the earth, and that every imagination of the thoughts of his heart was only evil continually' (Gen. 6:5). It certainly falls short of Jeremiah's charge: 'The heart is deceitful above all things, and desperately corrupt' (Jer. 17:9). Paul agrees — the sinner is not just wounded, but 'dead through ... trespasses and sins' (Eph. 2:1). He needs the miracle which produces 'a new creation' (2 Cor. 5:17).

Christ alone

The final words in this book must focus on the phrase which opened this chapter: 'justified by grace alone through faith alone in Christ alone' — concentrating on 'Christ alone'. It is his glory which is the matter of paramount importance, and his word which is to be our guide. This has lain behind the negatives which sadly have had to be registered. So Christ's unique status as the Second Person of the Trinity repudiates any attempt to make him first among equals. He is not simply one more religious teacher: he is 'the truth'. Also, while the miracle of his unique conception in the womb of the virgin is gladly asserted, a concern for his glory has led to resistance of any magnifying of claims for Mary which would place her in the area of sinlessness that is his alone. The same concern has led to a rejection of any idea that she could share at Calvary in the sacrifice which was uniquely his.

To see Christ as the Son who sends the Spirit as his vicar has led to a firm rejection of any promotion of priest or pope to be called either *'alter Christus'* (another Christ) or 'Supreme Pontiff' (high priest). The aim has been to point readers to the one perfect and sufficient sacrifice offered once and for all at Calvary. The allied aim has been to urge men and women to look in simple faith to Christ, and Christ alone.

In this life our understanding is imperfect and our pronouncements are fallible. But in heaven we shall no longer walk by faith but rather by sight. There the everlasting song of heaven will have as its dominant theme the glory of the Saviour (Rev. 1:6): 'To him who loves us and has freed us from our sins by his blood and made us a kingdom, priests to his God and Father, to him be glory and dominion for ever and ever. Amen.'

Bibliography

Main Roman Catholic sources

H. Roos S.J. and Joseph Neuner S.J., *The Teaching of the Catholic Church,* ed. Karl Rahner S.J. (The Mercier Press, 1966).

J. Neuner S.J. and J. Dupois S.J., eds, T*he Christian Faith* (The Mercier Press, 1973).

Walter M. Abbotts S.J., ed., D*ocuments of Vatican II* (Geoffrey Chapman, 1966).

Yves Conar O.P., Hans Küng and Daniel O'Hanlon S.J., eds, *Council Speeches of Vatican II* (Sheed & Ward, 1974).

Catechism of the Catholic Church (Geoffrey Chapman, 1994).

John Paul II, C*rossing the Threshold of Hope* (Jonathan Cape, 1994).

Encyclicals of the popes (various publishers)

A shortlist for further reading

(Roman Catholic titles are marked by an *)

Traditional Rome

G. C. Berkouwer, *The Conflict with Rome* (Presbyterian & Reformed, 1958).

*C. Butler, *The First Vatican Council* (Collins, 1962).

Henry Hudson, *Papal Power* (Evangelical Press, 1981).

W. S. Kerr, *A Handbook on the Papacy* (Marshall Morgan & Scott, 1962).

G. Miegge, T*he Virgin Mary* (Lutterworth, 1961).

*L. Ott, F*undamentals of Catholic Dogma* (Mercier, 1962).

G. Salmon, T*he Infallibility of the Church* (John Murray, 1914, abridged edition 1953)

V. Subilia, T*he Problem of Catholicism* (SCM, 1964).

W. Webster, *Salvation, the Bible and Roman Catholicism* (Banner of Truth, 1990)

Charismatic Rome

*Peter Hocken, *The Glory and the Shame* (Eagle, 1994).

*René Laurentin, *Catholic Pentecostalism* (Darton Longman & Todd, 1977)

*Edward O'Connor, *The Pentecostal Movement in the Catholic Church* (Ave Maria Press, 1971).

*Cardinal Suenens, *Ecumenism and Charismatic Renewal* (Darton Longman & Todd, 1978)

*Simon Tugwell, D*id you receive the Spirit?* (Darton Longman & Todd, 1972)

Radical Rome

G. C. Berkouwer, *The Second Vatican Council* (Eerdmans, 1965).

*A. M. J. Kloosterman, *Contemporary Catholicism* (Collins, 1972).

*Hans Küng, *The Church* (Burns & Oates, 1967).

*Hans Küng, *Justification* (Burns & Oates, 1964).

*Hans Küng, *Infallible?* (Collins, 1972).

*Hans Küng, *Why Priests?* (Collins, 1972).

Political Rome

A. Manhattan, *Vatican Imperialism and the Twentieth Century* (B. McCall Barbour/Zondervan, 1965).

Edmond Paris, *The Vatican against Europe,* translated from French (Protestant Truth Society, 1964).

Edmond Paris, *The Secret History of the Jesuits,* translated from French (Protestant Truth Society, 1975).

Michael de Semlyen, *All roads lead to Rome* (Dorchester, 1991).

David Yallop, *In God's Name* (Jonathan Cape, 1984).

History

Malachi Martin, *The Decline and Fall of the Roman Church* (Secker & Warburg, 1981).

L. Verduin, *The Anatomy of a Hybrid* (Eerdmans, 1976).

William Webster, *The Church of Rome at the Bar of History* (Banner of Truth, 1995).

Notes

Chapter 1 — Catechism of the Catholic Church
1. *Catechism of the Catholic Church* (Geoffrey Chapman, 1994), p.509, para, 1374, quoting Council of Trent, *Decree on the Most Holy Eucharist* (13th Session, ch. 1).
2. *Catechism*, p.432, para. 1989, quoting Trent, 6th Session, ch. 7.
3. *Catechism*, p.235, para. 1031.

Chapter 2 — History teaches us!
1. G. Miegge, *The Virgin Mary* (Lutterworth, 1961), p.86.
2. Quoted by W. S. Kerr in *A Handbook of the Papacy* (Marshall, Morgan & Scott, 1962), p.224.
3. *Annales Ecclesisatici: ann.* 912:8.
4. Reprinted as an appendix to *Papal Power* by Henry Hudson (Evangelical Press, 1981).
5. Kerr, *Handbook of the Papacy*, p.253.
6. Malachi Martin, *The Decline and Fall of the Roman Church* (Secker & Warburg, 1981), p.287.

Chapter 3 — Scripture and tradition
1. K. Rahner (ed.), *The Teaching of the Catholic Church* (The Mercier Press, 1966), p.59.
2. *Ibid.,* p.60.
3. *Ibid.,* p.63.
4. *Dogmatic Constitution on Divine Revelation,* II, 9,10.
5. *Ibid.,* II. 10.
6. *Decree on the Bishops' Pastoral Office in the Church,* II. 14.
7. *Catechism,* Article II. 82.
8. G. Salmon, *The Infallibility of the Church* (John Murray, 1914, abridged edition, 1953), p.143.

Chapter 4 — Infallible?
1. *Catechism,* p.205, para. 881.
2. *Catechism,* p. 125, para. 553.
3. Walter M. Abbott & J. Gallagher (eds), *Documents of Vatican II* (Geoffrey Chapman, 1966), *Lumen Gentium* 25.

4. *Catechism,* p.146, para. 641.
5. *Catechism,* p.205, para. 881.
6. *Catechism,* p.125, para. 553.

Chapter 5 — Radicals in Rome
1. Extracts from *'The New Inquisition?'* by Peter Hebblethwaite (Fount Paperbacks 1980) quoted in the *Guardian,* 5 April 1980.
2. Abbot & Gallagher (eds), *Documents of Vatican II,* p.715.
3. *Humani Generis,* para. 4.
4. K. M. McNamara (ed.), *Vatican II, The Constitution on the Church,* (Geoffrey Chapman 1968), p.157.
5. H. Küng, *Concilium,* IV 2 p.3.
6. *The Church is Mission* (Symposium, Geoffrey Chapman 1969), p.17.
7. *Ibid.,* p.13.

Chapter 6 — The church and the papacy
1. *Catechism,* p.173, para. 751.
2. Quoted in English translation by V. Subilia, *The Problem of Catholicism* (SCM, 1964), p.28.
3. *Mystici Corporis,* Part 1, para. 13.
4. *Ibid.,* Part I, para. 51.
5. Y. Congar, H. Küng & D. O'Hanlon (eds), *Council Speeches of Vatican II* (Sheed and Ward, 1974), p.12.
6. *Vatican II, Constitution on the Church (Lumen Gentium,* I.8).
7. *Catechism,* p.196, para. 846.
8. *Catechism,* p.440, para. 2030.
9. *Ibid.*
10. *Catechism,* p.200 para. 860.
11. H. Küng, *The Church* (Burns & Oates, 1967), pp.236,175.
12. The Nicene Creed.
13. For the whole sordid story of the Vatican Bank and the mysterious death of John Paul I in very suspicious circumstances, read *In God's name* by David Yallop (Jonathan Cape, 1984).

Chapter 7 — Catholic Pentecostalism
1. Cardinal Suenens, *Ecumenism and Charismatic Renewal* (Darton, Longman & Todd, 1978) pp.16-17.
2. *Ibid.,* p.29.
3. *Ibid.,* p.47.
4. *Ibid.,* p.90.
5. *Ibid.,* p.80.
6. Edward O'Connor, *The Pentecostal Movement in the Catholic Church* (Ave Maria Press, 1971), p.31.
7. Simon Tugwell, *Did you receive the Spirit?* (Darton, Longman & Todd, 1972), pp.87,99.
8. O'Connor, *The Pentecostal Movement in the Catholic Church,* pp.58ff.
9. René Laurentin, *Catholic Pentecostalism* (Darton, Longman & Todd, 1977), p.196.
10. *Ibid.,* p.193.

11. *Ibid.,* p.198.
12. *Mysterium Fidei,* paras 55-6.
13. Tugwell, *Did you receive the Spirit?*, p.42.
14. Kevin & Dorothy Ranaghan, *Catholic Pentecostals* (Paulist Press, 1969), pp.32,92,104.
15. O'Connor, *The Pentecostal Movement in the Catholic Church,* pp.127,167.
16. Suenens, *Ecumenism and Charismatic Renewal,* pp.78,90.
17. O'Connor, *The Pentecostal Movement in the Catholic Church,* p.256.
18. Peter Hocken, *The Glory and the Shame* (Eagle, 1994), p.194.

Chapter 8 — Mary
1. John Paul II, *Crossing the Threshold of Hope,* (Jonathan Cape, 1994), p.212.
2. *Ibid.,* p.215.
3. *Ibid.,* pp.220-21.
4. *To all the Bishops of the Church,* p.44.
5. *Catechesi Tradendæ,* pp.99,100.
6. *A Concilio Constaninopolitano* I
7. 'The Apparition at Knock': M. Walsh quoted by James Horan, parish priest of Knock, in a newspaper article.
8. *Everyman,* BBC 1, 'Mary's miracle', 18 December 1994.
9. *Catechism,* p.110, para. 493.
10. *Catechism,* p.220, para. 964.
11. *Vatican II — Lumen Gentium,* ch. 8 paras 56,58.
12. See Arndt and Gingrich, *Greek English Lexicon of the New Testament* .
13. *Vatican II — Lumen Gentium,* ch. 8, para. 61.
14. *Marialis Cultus,* p.82.
15. Encyclical Letter *Ad Diem Illum* (1904).

Chapter 9 — Why priests?
1. H. Küng, *Why Priests?* (Collins, 1972), p.19.
2. *Ibid.,* p.29.
3. *Catechism,* p.343, para. 1537.
4. 'A General Thanksgiving' in the *Book of Common Prayer.*
5. H. Küng, *Why Priests?,* p.43.
6. *Catechism,* p.249, para. 1084.
7. *Catechism,* p.258, para. 1127.
8. *Catechism,* para. 1128.
9. *Catechism,* p.259, para. 1129.
10. *Catechism,* p.277, para. 1215.
11. Tom. 1, p.488, Prag. 1721, quoted by Sydney Carter & Alison Weeks (eds), *The Protestant Dictionary* (Harrison Trust, 1933).
12. *Catechism,* p.258, para. 1127.

Chapter 10 — Penance and purgatory
1. *Catechism,* p.327, para. 1458.
2. Karl Rahner (ed.), *The Teaching of the Catholic Church* (Mercier Press, 1966), p.316.
3. *Catechism,* p.325, para. 1446.

4. *Catechism*, p.409, para. 1854.
5. *Catechism*, p.411, para. 1863.
6. *Catechism*, p.410, para. 1857.
7. *Catechism*, p.326, para. 1453.
8. *Catechism*, p.339, para. 1514.
9. *Catechism*, p.341, para. 1524.
10. *Catechism*, p.235, paras 1030-31.
11. Neuner & Depois, *The Christian Faith*, p.625.
12. *Ibid.*, p.627.
13. *Catechism*, p.331, para. 1471.
14. *Catechism*, p.332 para. 1477.
15. *Catechism*, p.219, para. 958.
16. *Catechism*, p.233, para. 1022.

11. Transubstantiation and the mass

1. Rahner (ed.), *The Teaching of the Catholic Church*, p.288.
2. *Ibid.*
3. *Ibid.*, pp.290-91.
4. *Constitution on the Sacred Liturgy*, ch.2, para. 55.
5. *Mysterium Fidei*, para. 55.
6. *The Holy Eucharist*, p.42.
7. *Ibid.*, p.9.
8. *Catechism*, p.309, para 1374.
9. Flynn, *The Charismatic Renewal and the Irish Experience*, pp.7,47.
10. Tugwell, *Did you Receive the Spirit?*, p.63.
11. Augustine, *The Third Book upon Christian Doctrine* (Benedictine Edition, 1685) III, p.52.
12. John Chrysostom, Homily XIV on 1 Corinthians.
13. Neuner & Dupuis, *The Christian Faith*, p.402.
14. *Ibid.*, p.403.
15. *Ibid.*, p.405.
16. *Mediator Dei*, para. 122.
17. *Decree on the priestly ministry and life*, ch. 2, para. 5.
18. *Mysterium Fidei*, para. 29
19. *The Holy Eucharist*, p.24.

Chapter 12 — Justified!

1. Council of Trent, ch. VII, decree 1528.
2. *Catechism*, p.432, para. 1987.
3. Hans Küng, *Justification* (Burns & Oates, 1964), p.106.
4. *Ibid.*, p.302.
5. *Ibid.*, p.303.
6. Council of Trent, decree 802.
7. Council of Trent, decree 808.
8. *Catechism*, p.325, para. 1446.
9. Council of Trent, canon 1959.
10. Council of Trent, canon 1692.
11. *Catechism*, p.91, para. 405.

Index